Mastering Play Framework for Scala

Leverage the awesome features of Play Framework to build scalable, resilient, and responsive applications

Shiti Saxena

PUBLISHING

BIRMINGHAM - MUMBAI

Mastering Play Framework for Scala

First published: May 2015

Production reference: 1260515

Published by Packt Publishing Ltd.
Livery Place
35 Livery Street
Birmingham B3 2PB, UK.

ISBN 978-1-78398-380-3

www.packtpub.com

Credits

Author

Shiti Saxena

Reviewers

Didier Bathily

Jérôme Leleu

Jon Parsons

Commissioning Editor

Amarabha Banerjee

Acquisition Editor

Subho Gupta

Content Development Editor

Sriram Neelakantan

Technical Editors

Novina Kewalramani

Manal Pednekar

Shruti Rawool

Copy Editors

Sonia Michelle Cheema

Vikrant Phadke

Project Coordinator

Vijay Kushlani

Proofreaders

Stephen Copestake

Safis Editing

Indexer

Monica Ajmera Mehta

Graphics

Sheetal Aute

Disha Haria

Production Coordinator

Arvindkumar Gupta

Cover Work

Arvindkumar Gupta

About the Author

Shiti Saxena is a software engineer with around 4 years of work experience. She is currently working with Imaginea (a business unit of Pramati). She has previously worked with Tata Consultancy Services Ltd. and Genpact.

A true polyglot, she's had exposure to various languages, including Scala, JavaScript, Java, Python, Perl, and C. She likes to work with Play Scala and AngularJS.

She blogs at `http://eraoferrors.blogspot.in` and maintains open source projects on GitHub.

She loves to travel, is a movie buff, and likes to spend time playing her piano whenever she is not programming.

She has authored *Getting Started with SBT for Scala* (`https://www.packtpub.com/application-development/getting-started-sbt-scala`).

Acknowledgments

I am indebted to my mother, Nithi, and my sisters, Shaila, Anshu, and Aastha, for their constant support. I am grateful to Aastha for helping me out with the images of this book.

A special thanks to my cousin Rohit for being there for me; he has guided, mentored, understood, and pampered me throughout. This book would not have been possible without his help. I would also like to thank his organization, Tuplejump.Inc, for giving me the idea of using real-time applications with Play Framework.

I'd like to thank Jay and Vijay Pullur for taking the initiative to start Pramati and everyone who's a part of it for making it a great place to work at.

I'd like to thank Apurba for believing in me and supporting me in my journey. I wouldn't have learned a lot of things if it wasn't for his guidance.

I'd also like to thank Guillaume Bort, Sadek Drobi, the Play Framework community, and Typesafe without whose efforts, bringing this technology to the forefront and writing this book wouldn't have been possible.

I am grateful to my friends for being there for me when I needed them.

A huge thanks to the team of Packt Publishing for coordinating and being patient with me when I wasn't able to meet their deadlines. I am also thankful to the reviewers, Didier, Jérôme, and Jon, for their valuable feedback, which has helped improve this book.

I would like to express my gratitude to everyone who has helped me reach this stage in my life. Thanks!

About the Reviewers

Didier Bathily is a Malian software engineer living in France, who founded an IT development company in 2011 with his friends (http://www.njin.fr).

His involvement in this field and passion for new technologies have given him some versatility in software development. Indeed, for customer's njin, he develops modern web applications in Scala / Play Framework, mobile applications for iOS or Android, and games for iOS or Mac OS X applications.

You can find him on GitHub at https://github.com/dbathily and on Twitter at https://twitter.com/dbathily.

Jérôme Leleu is a software architect living in Paris, France.

A consultant for 7 years, he has worked in many different companies and fields with different people. He has participated in many IT projects as a developer, technical lead, or projects manager, mostly involving J2EE technology.

Now, working in a French telecom company, he is the software architect of the web SSO, which supports very high traffic: millions of authentications from millions of users every day.

He is involved in open source development as a CAS (WebSSO) chairman. He is interested in security/protocol issues and has developed several libraries at http://www.pac4j.org to implement client support for protocols such as CAS, OAuth, and OpenID.

He is now the founder of an SSO cloud provider based on CAS (https://www.casinthecloud.com).

www.PacktPub.com

Support files, eBooks, discount offers, and more

For support files and downloads related to your book, please visit www.PacktPub.com.

Did you know that Packt offers eBook versions of every book published, with PDF and ePub files available? You can upgrade to the eBook version at www.PacktPub.com and as a print book customer, you are entitled to a discount on the eBook copy. Get in touch with us at service@packtpub.com for more details.

At www.PacktPub.com, you can also read a collection of free technical articles, sign up for a range of free newsletters and receive exclusive discounts and offers on Packt books and eBooks.

https://www2.packtpub.com/books/subscription/packtlib

Do you need instant solutions to your IT questions? PacktLib is Packt's online digital book library. Here, you can search, access, and read Packt's entire library of books.

Why subscribe?

- Fully searchable across every book published by Packt
- Copy and paste, print, and bookmark content
- On demand and accessible via a web browser

Free access for Packt account holders

If you have an account with Packt at www.PacktPub.com, you can use this to access PacktLib today and view 9 entirely free books. Simply use your login credentials for immediate access.

Table of Contents

Preface

The Play Framework is an open source web application framework that is written in Java and Scala. It follows the Model-View-Controller architectural pattern.

It enables the user to use Scala for application development, keeping key properties and features of the Play Framework intact. This results in faster and scalable web apps. Also, it uses a more functional and "Scala idiomatic" style of programming, without sacrificing simplicity and developer friendliness.

This book will provide advanced information on developing Scala web applications using the Play Framework. This will help Scala web developers master Play 2.0 and use it for pro-Scala web app development.

What this book covers

Chapter 1, Getting Started with Play, explains how to build simple applications using the Play Framework. We also explore the project structure so that you can understand how the framework plugs in the required settings through a build file.

Chapter 2, Defining Actions, explains how we can define an application-specific action with default parsers and results, and also with custom parsers and results.

Chapter 3, Building Routes, is where we see how essential routing is in a Play application. Apart from this, we also check out various default methods that Play provides for simplifying the process of routing.

Chapter 4, Exploring Views, explains how to create views using Twirl and the various other helper methods provided by Play. In this chapter, you also learn how you can support multiple languages in your Play application using the built-in i18n API.

Chapter 5, *Working with Data*, demonstrates different ways of causing application data to persist in an application that we build using the Play Framework. In addition to this, you also get to understand how the Play Cache API can be used and how it works.

Chapter 6, *Reactive Data Streams*, discusses the concepts of Iteratee, Enumerator, and Enumeratee and how they can be implemented in the Play Framework and used internally.

Chapter 7, *Playing with Globals*, gives an insight into the features provided for a Play application through the global plugin. We also discuss hooks for the request-response life cycle, using which we can intercept requests and responses and modify them if required.

Chapter 8, *WebSockets and Actors*, briefly covers the Actor Model and the usage of Akka Actors in an application. We also define a WebSocket connection in a Play application with various constraints and requirements, using different approaches.

Chapter 9, *Testing*, shows you how a Play application can be tested using Specs2 and ScalaTest. We go through the different helper methods available for simplifying testing of a Play application.

Chapter 10, *Debugging and Logging*, is where we configure the debugging of a Play application in the IDE. In this chapter, you get to learn how to start a Play application in the Scala console. This chapter also places emphasis on the logging API provided by the Play Framework and the methods of customizing the log format.

Chapter 11, *Web Services and Authentication*, explains the WS (WebService) plugin and the API exposed through it. We also access users' data from the service providers using OpenID and OAuth 1.0a.

Chapter 12, *Play in Production*, explains how to deploy a Play application on production. While deploying the application, we also check the different packaging options (RPM, Debian, ZIP, Windows, and so on) available by default.

Chapter 13, *Writing Play Plugins*, gives an explanation of all plugins, with their declaration, definition, and best practices.

What you need for this book

Before starting with this book, make sure that you have all of the necessary software installed. The prerequisites for this book are as follows:

- Java: http://www.oracle.com/technetwork/java/javase/downloads/jdk7-downloads-1880260.html

- **SBT or Activator:** `https://typesafe.com/community/core-tools/activator-and-sbt`
- **MariaDB:** `https://downloads.mariadb.org/`
- **MongoDB:** `http://www.mongodb.org/downloads`
- **Cassandra (optional):** `http://cassandra.apache.org/download/`

Who this book is for

This book is intended for those developers who are keen on mastering the internal working of Play Framework to effectively build and deploy web-related apps. It is assumed that you have a basic understanding of the core app development techniques.

Conventions

In this book, you will find a number of text styles that distinguish between different kinds of information. Here are some examples of these styles and an explanation of their meaning.

Code words in text, database table names, folder names, filenames, file extensions, pathnames, dummy URLs, user input, and Twitter handles are shown as follows: "Update the index template so that each `<li>` element has a button, clicking on which results in a delete request to the server."

A block of code is set as follows:

```
def running[T](app: Application)(block: => T): T = {
    synchronized {
      try {
        Play.start(app)
        block
      } finally {
        Play.stop()
      }
    }
}
```

When we wish to draw your attention to a particular part of a code block, the relevant lines or items are set in bold:

```
class WebSocketChannel(out: ActorRef)
  extends Actor with ActorLogging {

  val backend = Akka.system.actorOf(DBActor.props)
  def receive: Actor.Receive = {
    case jsRequest: JsValue =>
      backend ! convertJsonToMsg(jsRequest)
    case x:DBResponse =>
      out ! x.toJson
  }
}
```

Any command-line input or output is written as follows:

```
> run
[info] Compiling 1 Scala source to /AkkaActorDemo/target/scala-2.10/
classes...
[info] Running com.demo.Main
?od u od woH ,olleH
ekops ew ecnis gnoL neeB
Sorry, didn't quite understand that I can only process a String.
```

New terms and **important words** are shown in bold. Words that you see on the screen, for example, in menus or dialog boxes, appear in the text like this: "The form is not submitted when you click on **Submit**, and no errors are displayed using `globalErrors`."

 Warnings or important notes appear in a box like this.

 Tips and tricks appear like this.

Reader feedback

Feedback from our readers is always welcome. Let us know what you think about this book—what you liked or disliked. Reader feedback is important for us as it helps us develop titles that you will really get the most out of.

To send us general feedback, simply e-mail us at feedback@packtpub.com, and mention the book's title in the subject of your message.

If there is a topic that you have expertise in and you are interested in either writing or contributing to a book, see our author guide at www.packtpub.com/authors.

Customer support

Now that you are the proud owner of a Packt book, we have a number of things to help you to get the most from your purchase.

Downloading the example code

You can download the example code files from your account at http://www.packtpub.com for all the Packt Publishing books you have purchased. If you purchased this book elsewhere, you can visit http://www.packtpub.com/support and register to have the files e-mailed directly to you.

Errata

Although we have taken every care to ensure the accuracy of our content, mistakes do happen. If you find a mistake in one of our books—maybe a mistake in the text or the code—we would be grateful if you could report this to us. By doing so, you can save other readers from frustration and help us improve subsequent versions of this book. If you find any errata, please report them by visiting http://www.packtpub.com/submit-errata, selecting your book, clicking on the **Errata Submission Form** link, and entering the details of your errata. Once your errata are verified, your submission will be accepted and the errata will be uploaded to our website or added to any list of existing errata under the Errata section of that title.

To view the previously submitted errata, go to https://www.packtpub.com/books/content/support and enter the name of the book in the search field. The required information will appear under the **Errata** section.

Piracy

Piracy of copyrighted material on the Internet is an ongoing problem across all media. At Packt, we take the protection of our copyright and licenses very seriously. If you come across any illegal copies of our works in any form on the Internet, please provide us with the location address or website name immediately so that we can pursue a remedy.

Please contact us at copyright@packtpub.com with a link to the suspected pirated material.

We appreciate your help in protecting our authors and our ability to bring you valuable content.

Questions

If you have a problem with any aspect of this book, you can contact us at questions@packtpub.com, and we will do our best to address the problem.

1
Getting Started with Play

The World Wide Web has grown by leaps and bounds since its first appearance in August 1991. It has come a long way from line mode browsers and static websites to graphical browsers and highly interactive websites, such as search engines, online department stores, social networking, gaming, and so on.

Complex websites or applications are backed by one or more databases and several lines of code. In most cases, such web applications use a framework to simplify the development process. A framework provides a skeleton structure that handles most of the repetitive or common features. Ruby on Rails, Django, Grails, and Play are a few examples of this.

Play Framework was developed by Guillaume Bort while he was working at Zenexity (now Zengularity). Its first full release was in October 2009 for version 1.0. In 2011, Sadek Drobi joined Guillaume Bort to develop Play 2.0, which was adopted by Typesafe Stack 2.0. Play 2.0 was released on March 13, 2012.

In this chapter, we will be covering the following topics:

- The reasons for choosing Play
- Creating a sample Play application
- Creating a TaskTracker application

Venturing into the world of Play

Play's installation is hassle free. If you have Java JDK 6 or a later version, all you need to do to get Play working is an installation of **Typesafe Activator** or **Simple Build Tool (SBT)**.

Play is fully RESTful! **Representational State Transfer (REST)** is an architectural style, which relies on a stateless, client-server, and cache-enabled communication protocol. It's a lightweight alternative to mechanisms such as **Remote Procedure Calls (RPC)** and web services (which include SOAP, WSDL, and so on). Here stateless means that the client state data is not stored on the server and every request should include all the data required for the server to process it successfully. The server does not rely on previous data to process the current request. The clients store their session state and the servers can service many more clients in a stateless fashion. The Play build system uses **Simple Build Tool (SBT)**, which is a build tool used for Scala and Java. It also has a plugin to allow native compilation of C and C++. SBT uses incremental recompilation to reduce the compilation time and can be run in triggered execution mode, which means that if specified by the user, required tasks will be run whenever the user saves changes in any of the source files. This feature in particular has been leveraged by the Play Framework so that developers need not redeploy after every change in development stage. This means that if a Play app is running from source on your local machine and you edit its code, you can view the updated app just by reloading the app in the browser.

It provides a default test framework along with helpers and application stubs to simplify both unit and functional testing of the application. **Specs2** is the default testing framework used in Play.

Play comes with a Scala-based template engine, due to which it is possible to use Scala objects (`String`, `List`, `Map`, `Int`, user-defined objects, and so on) in the templates. This was not possible prior to 2.0 because earlier versions of Play relied on Groovy for the template engine.

It uses JBoss Netty as the default web server but any Play 2 application can be packaged as a WAR file and deployed on Servlet 2.5, 3.0, and 3.1 containers, if required. There is a plugin called **play2-war-plugin** (it can be found at `https://github.com/play2war/play2-war-plugin/`), which can be used to generate the WAR file for any given Play2 app.

Play endorses the **Model-View-Controller (MVC)** pattern. According to the MVC pattern, the components of an application can be divided into three categories:

- **Model**: This represents application data or activity
- **View**: This is the part of the application which is visible to the end user
- **Controller**: This is responsible for processing input from the end user

The pattern also defines how these components are supposed to interact with one another. Let's consider an online store as our application. In this case, the products, brands, users, cart, and so on can be represented by a model each. The pages in the application where users can view the products are defined in the views (HTML pages). When a user adds a product to the cart, the transaction is handled by a controller. The view is unaware of the model and the model is unaware of the view. The controller sends commands to the model and view. The following figure shows how the models, views, and controllers interact:

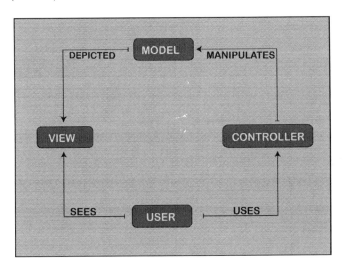

Play also comes prepackaged with an easy to use Hibernate layer, and offers OpenID, Ehcache, and web service integration straight out of the box by adding a dependency on the individual modules.

In the following sections of this chapter, we'll make a simple app using Play. This is mainly for developers who are using Play earlier.

A sample Play app

There are two ways of creating a new Play application: Activator, and without using Activator. It is simpler to create a Play project using Activator since the most minimalist app would require at least six files.

Typesafe Activator is a tool that can be used to create applications using the Typesafe stack. It relies on using predefined templates to create new projects. The instructions for setting up Activator can be found at `http://typesafe.com/get-started`.

Building a Play application using Activator

Let's build a new Play application using Activator and a simple template:

```
$ activator new pathtoNewApp/sampleApp just-play-scala
```

Then, run the project using the `run` command:

```
sampleApp $ sbt run
```

This starts the application, which is accessible at `http://localhost:9000`, by default.

 The `run` command starts the project in development mode. In this mode, the source code of the application is watched for changes, and if there are any changes the code is recompiled. We can then make changes to the models, views, or controllers and see them reflected in the application by reloading the browser.

Take a look at the project structure. It will be similar to the one shown here:

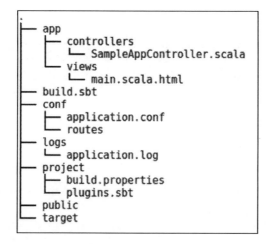

```
├── app
│   ├── controllers
│   │   └── SampleAppController.scala
│   └── views
│       └── main.scala.html
├── build.sbt
├── conf
│   ├── application.conf
│   └── routes
├── logs
│   └── application.log
├── project
│   ├── build.properties
│   └── plugins.sbt
├── public
└── target
```

If we can't use Activator, we will probably have to create all these files. Now, let's dig into the files individually and see which is for what purpose.

The build definition

Let's start with the crucial part of the project—its build definition, and in our case, the `build.sbt` file. The `.sbt` extension comes from the build tool used for Play applications. We will go through the key concepts of this for anyone who isn't familiar with SBT. The build definition is essentially a list of keys and their corresponding values, more or less like assignment statements with the `:=` symbol acting as the assignment operator.

SBT version lower than 0.13.7 expects a new line as the delimiter between two different statements in the build definition.

The contents of the build file are:

```
name := "sampleApp"""

version := "1.0.0"

lazy val root = project.in(file(".")).enablePlugins(PlayScala)
```

In the preceding build definition, the values for the project's `name`, `version`, and `root` are specified. Another way of specifying values is by updating the existing ones. We can append to the existing values using the `+=` symbol for individual items and `++=` for sequences. For example:

```
resolvers += Resolver.sonatypeRepo("snapshots")

scalacOptions ++= Seq("-feature", "-language:reflectiveCalls")
```

`resolvers` is the list of URLs from where the dependencies can be picked up and `scalacOptions` is the list of parameters passed to the Scala compiler.

Alternatively, an SBT project can also use a `.scala` build file. The structure for our application would then be:

```
├── app
│   ├── controllers
│   │   └── SampleAppController.scala
│   └── views
│       └── main.scala.html
├── conf
│   ├── application.conf
│   └── routes
├── logs
│   └── application.log
├── project
│   ├── build.properties
│   ├── plugins.sbt
│   └── SampleAppBuild.scala
├── public
└── target
```

The `.scala` build definition for `SimpleApp` will be:

```scala
import sbt._
import Keys._
import play.Play.autoImport._
import PlayKeys._

object ApplicationBuild extends Build {

  val appName = "SimpleApp"
  val appVersion = "1.0.0"


  val appDependencies = Seq(
    // Add your project dependencies here
  )

  val main = Project(appName,
    file(".")).enablePlugins(play.PlayScala).settings(
    version := appVersion,
    libraryDependencies ++= appDependencies
  )

}
```

The `.scala` build definition comes in handy when we need to define custom tasks/settings for our application/plugin, since it uses Scala code. The `.sbt` definition is generally smaller and simpler than its corresponding `.scala` definition and is hence, more preferred.

Without the Play settings, which are imported by enabling the PlayScala plugin, SBT is clueless that our project is a Play application and is defined according to the semantics of a Play application.

So, is that statement sufficient for SBT to run a Play app correctly?

No, there is something else as well! SBT allows us to extend build definitions using plugins. Play-based projects make use of the Play SBT plugin and it is from this plugin that SBT gets the required settings. In order for SBT to download all the plugins that our project will be using, they should be added explicitly. This is done by adding them in `plugins.sbt` in the `projectRoot/project` directory.

Let's take a look at the `plugins.sbt` file. The file content will be:

```
resolvers += "Typesafe repository" at
  "http://repo.typesafe.com/typesafe/releases/"

addSbtPlugin("com.typesafe.play" % "sbt-plugin" % "2.3.8")
```

The parameter passed to `addSbtPlugin` is the Ivy module ID for the plugin. The resolver is helpful when the plugin is not hosted on Maven or Typesafe repositories.

The `build.properties` file is used to specify the SBT version to avoid incompatibility issues between the same build definitions compiled by using two or more different versions of SBT.

This covers all the build-related files of a Play application.

The source code

Now, let us look at the source code for our project. Most of the source is in the `app` folder. Generally, the model's code is within `app/models` or `app/com/projectName/models` and the controller's source code is in `app/controllers` or `app/com/projectName/controllers`, where `com.projectName` is the package. The code for the views should be in `app/views` or within a subfolder in `app/views`.

The `views/main.scala.html` file is the page we will be able to see when we run our application. If this file is missing, you can add it. If you are wondering why the file is named `main.scala.html` and not `main.html`, this is because it's a Twirl template; it facilitates using Scala code along with HTML to define views. We will delve deeper into this in *Chapter 4, Exploring Views*.

Now, update the content of `main.scala.html` to:

```
@(title: String)(content: Html)

<!DOCTYPE html>

<html>
    <head>
        <title>@title</title>
    </head>
    <body>
    @content
    </body>
</html>
```

We can provide the title and content from our Scala code to display this view. A view can be bound to a specific request through the controllers. So, let's update the code for our controller `SampleAppController`, as follows:

```
package controllers

import play.api.mvc._
import play.api.templates.Html

object SampleAppController extends Controller {
  def index = Action {
    val content = Html("<div>This is the content for the sample
      app<div>")
        Ok(views.html.main("Home")(content))
  }
}
```

Downloading the example code

You can download the example code files for all Packt books you have purchased from your account at `http://www.packtpub.com`. If you purchased this book elsewhere, you can visit `http://www.packtpub.com/support` and register to have the files e-mailed directly to you.

`Action` and `Ok` are methods made available by the `play.mvc.api` package. *Chapter 2, Defining Actions* covers them in detail.

On saving the changes and running the application, we will see the page hosted at `http://localhost:9000`, as shown in the screenshot:

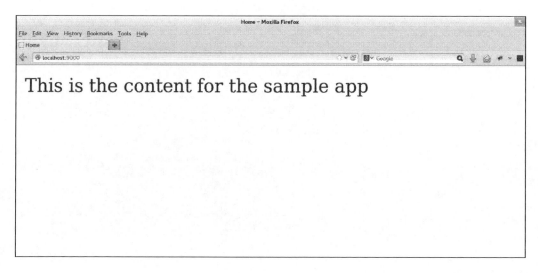

Request handling process

Let's see how the request was handled!

All requests that will be supported by the application must be defined in the `conf/routes` file. Each route definition has three parts. The first part is the request method. It can be any one of `GET`, `POST`, `PUT`, and `DELETE`. The second part is the path and the third is the method, which returns a response. When a request is defined in the `conf/routes` file, the method to which it is mapped in the `conf/routes` file is called.

For example, an entry in the routes file would be:

```
GET            /                           controllers.SampleAppController.
index
```

This means that for a GET request on the / path, we have mapped the response to be the one returned from the `SampleController.index()` method.

A sample request would be:

```
curl 'http://localhost:9000/'
```

Go ahead and add a few more pages to the application to get more comfortable, maybe a FAQ, Contact Us, or About.

The request-response cycle for a Play app, explained in the preceding code is represented here:

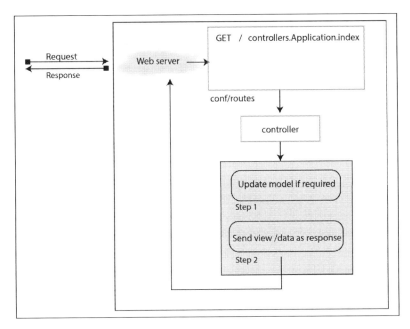

The `public` directory is essentially used to serve resources, such as stylesheets, JavaScript, and images that are independent of Play. To make these files accessible, the path to `public` is also added in routes by default:

```
GET          /assets/*file              controllers.Assets.at(path="/
public", file)
```

We will see routes in detail in *Chapter 3, Building Routes*.

The file `conf/application.conf` is used to set application-level configuration properties.

The `target` directory is used by SBT for the files generated during compile, build, or other processes.

Creating a TaskTracker application

Let us create a simple **TaskTracker** application, which allows us to add pending tasks and delete them. We will continue by modifying `SampleApp`, built in the previous section. In this app, we will not be using a DB to store the tasks. It is possible to persist models in Play using **Anorm** or other modules; this is discussed in more detail in *Chapter 5, Working with Data*.

We need a view that has an input box to enter the task. Add another template file, `index.scala.html`, to the views, using the template generated in the preceding section as boilerplate:

```
@main("Task Tracker") {

    <h2>Task Tracker</h2>

    <div>
        <form>
        <input type="text" name="taskName" placeholder="Add a new
          Task" required>

        <input type="submit" value="Add">
        </form>
    </div>

}
```

In order to use a template, we can call its generated method from our Scala code or refer to it in other templates by using its name. Using a main template can come in handy when we want to apply a change to all the templates. For example, if we want to add a style sheet for an application, just adding this in our main template will ensure that it's added for all the dependent views.

To view this template's content on loading, update the `index` method to:

```
package controllers

import play.api.mvc._

object TaskController extends Controller {
  def index = Action {
    Ok(views.html.index())
  }
}
```

Notice that we have also replaced all occurrences of `SampleAppController` to `TaskController`.

Run the application and view it in the browser; the page will look similar to this figure:

Now, in order to work on the functionality, let's add a model called `Task`, which we'll use to represent the task in our app. Since we want to delete the functionality too, we will need to identify each task using a unique ID, which means that our model should have two properties: an ID and a name. The `Task` model will be:

```
package models

case class Task(id: Int, name: String)

object Task {

  private var taskList: List[Task] = List()

  def all: List[Task] = {
    taskList
```

```
    }

    def add(taskName: String) = {
       val newId: Int = taskList.last.id + 1
       taskList = taskList ++ List(Task(newId, taskName))
    }

    def delete(taskId: Int) = {
       taskList = taskList.filterNot(task => task.id == taskId)
    }
}
```

In this model, we are using a `taskList` private variable to keep track of the tasks for the session.

In the `add` method, whenever a new task is added, we append it to this list. Instead of keeping another variable to keep count of the IDs, I choose to increment the ID of the last element in the list.

In the `delete` method, we simply filter out the task with the given ID and the `all` method returns the list for this session.

Now, we need to call these methods in our controller and then bind them to a request route. Now, update the controller in this way:

```
import models.Task
import play.api.mvc._

object TaskController extends Controller {

   def index = Action {
      Redirect(routes.TaskController.tasks)
   }

   def tasks = Action {
      Ok(views.html.index(Task.all))
   }

   def newTask = Action(parse.urlFormEncoded) {
      implicit request =>
         Task.add(request.body.get("taskName").get.head)
         Redirect(routes.TaskController.index)
   }

   def deleteTask(id: Int) = Action {
```

```
    Task.delete(id)
    Ok
  }

}
```

In the preceding code, `routes` refers to the helper that can be used to access the routes defined for the application in `conf/routes`. Try running the app now!

It'll throw a compilation error, which says that values tasks is not a member of `controllers.ReverseTaskController`. This occurs because we haven't yet updated the routes.

Adding a new task

Now, let's bind actions to get tasks and add a new task:

```
GET             /                    controllers.TaskController.index

# Tasks
GET             /tasks               controllers.TaskController.tasks
POST            /tasks               controllers.TaskController.newTask
```

We'll complete our application's view so that it can facilitate the following:

```
accept and render a List[Task]

  @(tasks: List[Task])

  @main("Task Tracker") {

      <h2>Task Tracker</h2>
      <div>
          <form action="@routes.TaskController.newTask()"
            method="post">
              <input type="text" name="taskName" placeholder="Add a
                new Task" required>
              <input type="submit" value="Add">
          </form>
      </div>
      <div>
          <ul>
          @tasks.map { task =>
              <li>
                  @task.name
              </li>
```

```
        }
    </ul>
  </div>
}
```

We have now added a form in the view, which takes a text input with the `taskName` name and submits this data to a `TaskController.newTask` method.

 Notice that we have now added a `tasks` argument for this template and are displaying it in the view. Scala elements and predefined templates are prepended with the @ twirl symbol in the views.

Now, when running the app, we will be able to add tasks as well as view existing ones, as shown here:

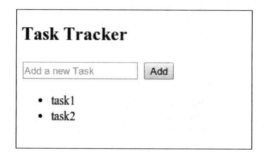

Deleting a task

The only thing remaining in our app is the ability to delete a task. Update the index template so that each `<li>` element has a button, whose click results in a delete request to the server:

```
<li>
    @task.name <button onclick="deleteTask ( @task.id)
        ;">Remove</button>
</li>
```

Then, we would need to update the routes file to map the delete action:

```
DELETE        /tasks/:id            controllers.TaskController.deleteTask
  (id: Int).
```

We also need to define `deleteTask` in our view. To do this, we can simply add a script:

```
<script>
function deleteTask ( id ) {
```

```
    var req = new XMLHttpRequest ( ) ;
    req.open ( "delete", "/tasks/" + id ) ;
    req.onload = function ( e ) {
        if ( req.status = 200 ) {
            document.location.reload ( true ) ;
        }
    } ;
    req.send ( ) ;


}
</script>
```

 Ideally, we shouldn't be defining JavaScript methods in the window's global namespace. It has been done in this example, so as to keep it simple and it's not advised for any real-time application.

Now, when we run the app, we can add tasks as well as remove them, as shown here:

I am leaving the task of beautifying the app up to you. Add a style sheet in the public directory and declare it in the main template. For example, if the `taskTracker.css` file is located at `public/stylesheets`, the link to it in the `main.scala.html` file would be:

```
<link rel="stylesheet" media="screen"
  href="@routes.Assets.at("stylesheets/taskTracker.css")">
```

Summary

This chapter gives a basic introduction to the Play Framework. In this chapter, we have learned how to build simple applications using the Play Framework. We have gone through its project structure to understand how the framework plugs in required settings through the build file. We have also discussed the various bits and pieces of such applications: models, routes, views, controllers, and so on.

In the next chapter, we will cover actions in detail.

2
Defining Actions

If you're reading this, you've either survived the first chapter or skipped it. Either way, I am assuming you know the structure of a simple Play application. A controller in Play generates Action values and, to do so, it uses several objects and methods internally. In this chapter, we will see what goes on behind the scenes and how we can leverage these actions when we build our application.

In this chapter, we will be covering the following topics:

- Defining Actions
- Request body parsers
- Action composition and troubleshooting

A dummy Artist model

In the following sections, we will give make reference to an `artist` model. It is a simple `class` with a companion `object`, defined as follows:

```scala
case class Artist(name: String, country: String)

object Artist {
  val availableArtist = Seq(Artist("Wolfgang Amadeus Mozart",
    "Austria"),
    Artist("Ludwig van Beethoven", "Germany"),
    Artist("Johann Sebastian Bach", "Germany"),
    Artist("Frédéric François Chopin", "Poland"),
    Artist("Joseph Haydn", "Austria"),
    Artist("Antonio Lucio Vivaldi", "Italy"),
    Artist("Franz Peter Schubert", "Austria"),
    Artist("Franz Liszt", "Austria"),
```

```
      Artist("Giuseppe Fortunino Francesco Verdi", "Austria"))

  def fetch: Seq[Artist] = {
    availableArtist
  }


  def fetchByName(name: String): Seq[Artist] = {
    availableArtist.filter(a => a.name.contains(name))
  }


  def fetchByCountry(country: String): Seq[Artist] = {
    availableArtist.filter(a => a.country == country)
  }


  def fetchByNameOrCountry(name: String, country: String):
    Seq[Artist] = {
    availableArtist.filter(a => a.name.contains(name) || a.country
      == country)
  }


  def fetchByNameAndCountry(name: String, country: String):
    Seq[Artist] = {
    availableArtist.filter(a => a.name.contains(name) && a.country
      == country)
  }
}
```

The Artist model has a method to fetch all these artists and a few methods to filter the artist, based on different parameters.

 In real applications, the model interacts with the database but to keep things simple, we have hardcoded the data as Seq[Artist].

We also have a view of home.scala.html, which displays information about the artist in a table:

```
@(artists: Seq[Artist])
<!DOCTYPE html>

<html>
    <head>
        <title>Action App</title>
    </head>
    <body>
```

```
<table>
    <thead>
        <tr>
            <th>Name</th>
            <th>Country</th>
            </tr>
    </thead>
    <tbody>
    @artists.map { artist =>
        <tr>
            <td>@artist.name</td>
            <td>@artist.country</td>
        </tr>
    }
    </tbody>
</table>
</body>
</html>
```

This is a twirl, template which requires a Seq[Artist]. It is similar to the view of the TaskTracker application we built in the previous chapter.

Actions

An **Action** in Play defines how a server should respond to a request. The methods, which define an Action, are mapped to a request in the routes file. For example, let's define an Action which displays the information of all the artists as a response:

```
def listArtist = Action {
  Ok(views.html.home(Artist.fetch))
}
```

Now, to use this Action, we should map it to a request in the routes file.

```
GET      /api/artist          controllers.Application.listArtist
```

In this example, we fetch all the artists and send them with the view, as the response to the request.

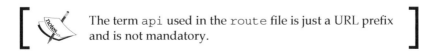

The term api used in the route file is just a URL prefix and is not mandatory.

Run the application and access http://localhost:9000/api/artist from the browser. A table with the available artist is visible.

Action takes a request and yields a result. It is an implementation of the `EssentialAction` trait. It is defined as:

```
trait EssentialAction extends (RequestHeader =>
  Iteratee[Array[Byte], Result]) with Handler {

  def apply() = this

}


object EssentialAction {
  def apply(f: RequestHeader => Iteratee[Array[Byte], Result]):
    EssentialAction = new EssentialAction {
    def apply(rh: RequestHeader) = f(rh)
  }
}
```

Iteratee is a concept borrowed from functional languages. It is used to process chunks of data in an incremental manner. We will dig deeper into it in *Chapter 6, Reactive Data Streams*.

The apply method accepts a function, which transforms a request into a result. The `RequestHeader` and other chunks of data represent the request. In short, the `apply` method takes in a request and returns a result.

Let's see some of the ways in which an action can be defined.

Actions with parameters

We might come across a situation where we need to define an Action, which takes a value from the request path. In this case, we will need to add the parameters required for the method signature and pass them in the routes file. An example of this would be the method to fetch artists by their selected names. In the controller, add the following:

```
def fetchArtistByName(name:String) = Action {
  Ok(views.html.home(Artist.fetchByName(name)))
}
```

The mapping for this in the `routes` file will be:

```
GET     /api/artist/:name       controllers.Application.
fetchArtistByName(name)
```

If it's not specified explicitly, keep in mind that the type of parameter in the path is set to `String` by default. The type can be specified in the method call. So, the route defined is equivalent to:

```
GET     /api/artist/:name           controllers.
Application.fetchArtistByName(name:String)
```

Similarly, we could add more parameters if required.

Now, take the use case of a search query. We want the action to accept query parameters, such as name and country. The action is defined as:

```
def search(name: String, country: String) = Action {
    val result = Artist.fetchByNameOrCountry(name, country)
    if(result.isEmpty){
      NoContent
       }
    else {
      Ok(views.html.home(result))
    }
  }
```

If there are no artists matching the criteria, the response is empty, and shows a status code 204 (no content). If it doesn't, the response status is `200 = (Ok)`, and shows the result as the response body.

The entry corresponding to this Action in the routes file will be the following:

```
GET     /api/search/artist          controllers.Application.search(name:S
tring,country:String)
```

We do not use any parameters in the path, but query parameters whose labels correspond to the method's parameter names in the `routes` file should be included.

This will result in a valid URL: `http://localhost:9000/api/search/artist?name=Franz&country=Austria`

What if we decided to make `country` an optional parameter?

Let's modify the route to accommodate this change:

```
GET     /api/search/artist      controllers.Application.search(name:Strin
g?="",country:String?="")
```

This allows us to make queries by the name as well, so, both the URLs will now look like this: `http://localhost:9000/api/search/artist?name=Franz` and `http://localhost:9000/api/search/artist?name=Franz&country=Austria` are now supported.

Here, we made the `country` parameter optional by setting a default value for it in the route definition. Alternatively, we could define an Action to accept a parameter of the `Option` type:

```
def search2(name: Option[String], country: String) = Action {
    val result = name match{
      case Some(n) => Artist.fetchByNameOrCountry(n, country)
      case None => Artist.fetchByCountry(country)
    }
    if(result.isEmpty){
      NoContent
    }
    else {
      Ok(views.html.home(result))
    }
}
```

Then, the route will be as follows:

```
GET    /api/search2/artist    controllers.Application.search2(name:Opt
ion[String],country:String
)
```

We can now make requests with or without passing the name of the country:

`http://localhost:9000/api/search2/artist?country=Austria`

`http://localhost:9000/api/search2/artist?name=Franz&country=Austria`

In the examples shown in this section, we didn't need to use the request to generate our result but in some cases, we would use the request to generate a relevant result. However, to do this, understanding the format of the request content is crucial. We'll see how this is done in the following section.

Request body parsers

Consider the most common POST request in any application—the request sent for logins. Will it be sufficient if the request body has the user's credentials in, say, a JSON or XML format? Will the request handler be able to extract this data and process it directly? No, since the data in the request has to be understood by the application code, it must be translated into a compatible type. For example, XML sent in a request must be translated to Scala XML for a Scala application.

There are several libraries, such as Jackson, XStream, and so on, which can be used to achieve this task, but we wouldn't need them as Play supports this internally. Play provides request body parsers to transform the request body into equivalent Scala objects for some of the frequently used content types. In addition to this, we can extend existing parsers or define new ones.

Every Action has a parser. How do I know this ? Well, the Action object, which we used to define how our app should respond, is simply an extension of the Action trait, and is defined as follows:

```
trait Action[A] extends EssentialAction {

//Type of the request body.
type BODY_CONTENT = A

//Body parser associated with this action.
def parser: BodyParser[A]

//Invokes this action
def apply(request: Request[A]): Future[Result]

    def apply(rh: RequestHeader): Iteratee[Array[Byte], Result] =
      parser(rh).mapM {
        case Left(r) =>

    Future.successful(r)
  case Right(a) =>
    val request = Request(rh, a)

    Play.maybeApplication.map { app =>
      play.utils.Threads.withContextClassLoader(app.classloader) {
        apply(request)
        }
    }.getOrElse {
       apply(request)
    }
```

```
} (executionContext)

//The execution context to run this action in
def executionContext: ExecutionContext =
  play.api.libs.concurrent.Execution.defaultContext

//Returns itself, for better support in the routes file.
override def apply(): Action[A] = this

override def toString = {
  "Action(parser="+ parser + ")"
}

}
```

The `apply` method transforms the value returned by the parser. The value from the parser can either be a result or the request body (denoted as `Either[Result,A]`).

Therefore, the transformation is defined for both possible outcomes. If we pattern-match this, we get `Left(r)`, which is a result type and `Right(a)`, which is the request body.

The `mapM` method functions similarly to the `map` method, the only difference being, it does so asynchronously.

However, can Actions be defined even without a parser? Yes and no.

Let's look at an example Action: a POST request, which is required to subscribe to updates. This request takes the user's e-mail ID as a query parameter, which means that we will need to access the request body in order to complete the subscription for this user. First, we'll check what the request body looks like when we do not specify a parser. Create an Action `subscribe` in a controller, as shown here:

```
def subscribe = Action {
    request =>
        Ok("received " + request.body)
    }
```

Now, add an entry for this in the routes file:

```
POST     /subscribe              controllers.AppController.subscribe
```

After this, run the application. Send a POST request at `http://localhost:9000/subscribe` with the `userId@gmail.com` e-mail ID using a REST client or Curl (whichever you are more comfortable with).

For example:

```
curl 'http://localhost:9000/subscribe' -H 'Content-Type:
   text/plain;charset=UTF-8' --data-binary 'userId@gmail.com'
```

The response for this request will be as follows:

```
received AnyContentAsText(userId@gmail.com)
```

Did you notice that our `subscribe` method understood that the content was text? The request body was translated as `AnyContentAsText(userId@gmail.com)`. How did our method determine this? Isn't this the job of a parser mapped to a particular Action?

When a parser is not specified for an Action, the parser returned by the `BodyParsers.parse.anyContent` method is set as the parser for this Action. This is handled by the `ActionBuilder`, which we will see later in this chapter. The following code snippet shows one of the methods to generate an Action when no parser is given:

```
final def apply(block: R[AnyContent] => Result):
   Action[AnyContent] = apply(BodyParsers.parse.anyContent)(block)
```

Now, let's examine what the `BodyParsers.parse.anyContent` method does:

```
def anyContent: BodyParser[ AnyContent] = BodyParser("anyContent")
  { request =>
     import play.api.libs.iteratee.Execution.Implicits.trampoline
     request.contentType.map(_.toLowerCase(Locale.ENGLISH)) match {
       case _ if request.method == HttpVerbs.GET ||
         request.method == HttpVerbs.HEAD => {
         Play.logger.trace("Parsing AnyContent as empty")
         empty(request).map(_.right.map(_ => AnyContentAsEmpty))
       }
       case Some("text/plain") => {
         Play.logger.trace("Parsing AnyContent as text")
         text(request).map(_.right.map(s => AnyContentAsText(s)))
       }
       case Some("text/xml") | Some("application/xml") |
         Some(ApplicationXmlMatcher()) => {
         Play.logger.trace("Parsing AnyContent as xml")
         xml(request).map(_.right.map(x => AnyContentAsXml(x)))
        }
       case Some("text/json") | Some("application/json") => {
         Play.logger.trace("Parsing AnyContent as json")
         json(request).map(_.right.map(j => AnyContentAsJson(j)))
       }
```

```
        case Some("application/x-www-form-urlencoded") => {
          Play.logger.trace("Parsing AnyContent as
            urlFormEncoded")
          urlFormEncoded(request).map(_.right.map(d =>
            AnyContentAsFormUrlEncoded(d)))
        }
        case Some("multipart/form-data") => {
          Play.logger.trace("Parsing AnyContent as
            multipartFormData")
          multipartFormData(request).map(_.right.map(m =>
            AnyContentAsMultipartFormData(m)))
        }
        case _ => {
          Play.logger.trace("Parsing AnyContent as raw")
          raw(request).map(_.right.map(r => AnyContentAsRaw(r)))
            }
        }
      }
```

First of all, it checks whether the request type supports sending data along with the request. If not, it returns `AnyContentAsEmpty` (you can check this by changing the request type to GET in the routes file and sending a GET request), else it compares the content type Header of the request with the supported types. If a match is found, it transforms the data into the corresponding type and returns that, or else it parses it as bytes and returns `play.api.mvc.RawBuffer`.

> `AnyContentAsEmpty, AnyContentAsText, AnyContentAsXml,`
> `AnyContentAsJson, AnyContentAsFormUrlEncoded,`
> `AnyContentAsMultipartFormData,` and `AnyContentAsRaw` all
> extend the trait `AnyContent`.

So, when an Action is defined for one of the supported content types or when it's a GET/HEAD request, we need not mention the parser.

Let's see how we can access the request body in our Action. We can now updating our `subscribe` method:

```
def subscribe = Action {
    request =>
      val reqBody: AnyContent = request.body
      val textContent: Option[String] = reqBody.asText
      textContent.map {
        emailId =>
          Ok("added " + emailId + " to subscriber's list")
      }.getOrElse {
```

```
        BadRequest("improper request body")
    }
}
```

In order to access the data in the request body, we need to convert it from `AnyContent` to `Option[String]` using the `asText` method. This would become more concise if we added the parser in the Action definition:

```
def subscribe = Action(parse.text) {
    request =>
      Ok("added " + request.body + " to subscriber's list")
}
```

The `urlFormEncoded` text XML parsers return standard Scala objects while the others return Play objects.

We can assume that the subscription request takes a JSON in this format:

```
{"emailId": "userId@gmail.com", " interval": "month"}
```

Now, we will need to modify our `subscribe` method to `def subscribe = Action(parse.json) {`, as shown here:

```
     request =>
    val reqData: JsValue = request.body
    val emailId = (reqData \ "emailId").as[String]
    val interval = (reqData \ "interval").as[String]
    Ok(s"added $emailId to subscriber's list and will send updates
every $interval")
  }
```

For the following request:

```
curl 'http://localhost:9000/subscribe' -H 'Content-Type:
  text/json' --data-binary '{"emailId": "userId@gmail.com",
  "interval": "month"}'
```

We get a response as follows:

Added `userId@gmail.com` to the subscriber's list and will send updates every month

The `parse.json` transforms the request body to `play.api.libs.json.JsValue`. The \ operator is used to access the value of a particular key. Similarly, there is a \\ operator, which can be for the value of a key, though it may not be a direct child of the current node. Play-Json has several methods that simplify the handling of data in a JSON format, such as modifying the structure, or converting it to Scala models, and so on. Play-Json is also available as a stand-alone library to enable its usage in non-Play projects. Its documentation is available at `https://www.playframework.com/documentation/2.3.x/ScalaJson`.

Now, let's see how to write an Action to add a new user, which takes a request of content-type multipart:

```
import java.io.File

def createProfile = Action(parse.multipartFormData) {
  request =>
    val formData = request.body.asFormUrlEncoded
    val email: String = formData.get("email").get(0)
    val name: String = formData.get("name").get(0)
    val userId: Long = User(email, name).save
    request.body.file("displayPic").map {
      picture =>
        val path = "/socialize/user/"
        if (!picture.filename.isEmpty) {
          picture.ref.moveTo(new File(path + userId + ".jpeg"))
        }
        Ok("successfully added user")
    }.getOrElse {
        BadRequest("failed to add user")
    }
}
```

The request has three fields: `email`, `name`, and `displayPic`. From the request data, we fetch the e-mail of, name, and add a new user. The `User.save` method adds an entry in the user table and throws an error if a user with the same e-mail ID exists. This is why the operations in the file are performed only after adding a user. The `displayPic` is optional; therefore, the check for its length to be greater than zero is made prior to saving the image.

It is better to complete the data transactions before the file-related ones, since they may fail and file-related operations might not be required for the incorrect request. The following table shows the supported content-types, parsers, and their default conversions.

Content type	Parser	Parsed to Scala type
`text/plain`	`text`	`String`
`application/json` or `text/json`	`json`	`play.api.libs.json.JsValue`
`application/xml`, `text/xml`, or `application/XXX+xml`	`xml`	`NodeSeq`
`application/form-url-encoded`	`urlFormEncoded`	`Map[String, Seq[String]]`
`multipart/form-data`	`multipartFormData`	`play.api.mvc.MultipartFormData[TemporaryFile]`
`other`	`raw`	`Play.api.mvc.RawBuffer`

Extending a parser

Let's extend the JSON parser so that we get a subscription model. We will assume that the `Subscription` model is defined as follows:

```
case class Subscription(emailId: String,
                        interval: String)
```

Now, let's write a parser that transforms the request body into a subscription object. The following code should be written in a controller:

```
val parseAsSubscription = parse.using {
    request =>
      parse.json.map {
        body =>
          val emailId:String = (body \ "emailId").as[String]
          val fromDate:Long = (body \ "fromDate").as[Long]
          Subscription(emailId, fromDate)
      }
}

implicit val subWrites = Json.writes[Subscription]
def getSub = Action(parseAsSubscription) {
```

```
    request =>
      val subscription: Subscription = request.body
      Ok(Json.toJson(subscription))
  }
```

There are also tolerant parsers. By tolerant, we mean that errors in a format are not ignored. This simply means that it ignores the content type header in the request and parses based on the type specified. For example, let's update the `subscribe` method:

```
def subscribe = Action(parse.tolerantJson) {
    request =>
      val reqData: JsValue = request.body
      val emailId = (reqData \ "email").as[String]
      val interval = (reqData \ "interval").as[String]
   Ok(s"added $emailId to subscriber's list and will send updates
      every $interval")
    }
```

Now, a request with the content type as text and a request where the content type text/JSON, or any other type for that matter, will give the same result. There are tolerant parsers for all the basic parsers supported in Play.

Exploring the results

In Play, the response to a request is a **result**. A result has two components: the response header and the response body. Let's look at a simple example of this:

```
def plainResult = Action {
  Result(
    header = ResponseHeader(200, Map(CONTENT_TYPE ->
      "text/plain")),
    body = Enumerator("This is the response from plainResult
      method".getBytes())
  )
}
```

Notice that we used an enumerator for the response body. An enumerator is a means to provide data to an iteratee. We will discuss these in detail in *Chapter 6, Reactive Data Streams*.

Apart from this, a result has additional functions that equips us with better means to handle response headers, sessions, cookies, and so on.

A result can send JSON, XML, and images as a response, apart from a String content. An easier way of generating a result is to use the result helpers. A result helper is used for most of the HTTP response status. As an example, let's see how the TODO Action that comes built in with Play is implemented:

```
val TODO = Action {
    NotImplemented[play.api.templates.Html](views.html.defaultpages.
todo())
    }
```

In this snippet, `NotImplemented` is a helper, which returns a result with a status of 501 and `views.html.defaultpages.todo()` returns the default page, which is `todo.scala.html`.

As an example, we'll consider the Action that sends the user's profile image inline. The Action would now be as follows:

```
def getUserImage(userId: Long) = Action {
    val path: String = s"/socialize/user/$userId.jpeg"
    val img = new File(path)
    if (img.exists()) {
      Ok.sendFile(
        content = img,
        inline = true
      )
    }
    else
      NoContent
    }
```

Here, we attempt to load the user's profile image using the predefined `getUserImagePath` method. If the image file exists and attaches itself to the response, we return a response with the 204 status code.

We also saw how a result helper can be used to send the page content, both static and dynamic, using views:

```
def listArtist = Action {
    Ok(views.html.home(Artist.fetch))

    }
```

We could also use the `Status` class to generate the result, as shown here:

```
def save = Action(parse.text) {
    request =>
      Status(200)("Got: " + request.body)
  }
```

This table shows you the result helpers and their corresponding status codes:

Result helper	Status code constants	Status code
–	CONTINUE	100
–	SWITCHING_PROTOCOLS	101
Ok	OK	200
Created	CREATED	201
Accepted	ACCEPTED	202
NonAuthoritativeInformation	NON_AUTHORITATIVE_ INFORMATION	203
NoContent	NO_CONTENT	204
ResetContent	RESET_CONTENT	205
PartialContent	PARTIAL_CONTENT	206
MultiStatus	MULTI_STATUS	207
–	MULTIPLE_CHOICES	300
MovedPermanently	MOVED_PERMANENTLY	301
Found	FOUND	302
SeeOther	SEE_OTHER	303
NotModified	NOT_MODIFIED	304
–	USE_PROXY	305
TemporaryRedirect	TEMPORARY_REDIRECT	307
BadRequest	BAD_REQUEST	400
Unauthorized	UNAUTHORIZED	401
–	PAYMENT_REQUIRED	402
Forbidden	FORBIDDEN	403
NotFound	NOT_FOUND	404
MethodNotAllowed	METHOD_NOT_ALLOWED	405
NotAcceptable	NOT_ACCEPTABLE	406
–	PROXY_AUTHENTICATION_ REQUIRED	407
RequestTimeout	REQUEST_TIMEOUT	408

Result helper	Status code constants	Status code
Conflict	CONFLICT	409
Gone	GONE	410
-	LENGTH_REQUIRED	411
PreconditionFailed	PRECONDITION_FAILED	412
EntityTooLarge	REQUEST_ENTITY_TOO_LARGE	413
UriTooLong	REQUEST_URI_TOO_LONG	414
UnsupportedMediaType	UNSUPPORTED_MEDIA_TYPE	415
-	REQUESTED_RANGE_NOT_SATISFIABLE	416
ExpectationFailed	EXPECTATION_FAILED	417
UnprocessableEntity	UNPROCESSABLE_ENTITY	422
Locked	LOCKED	423
FailedDependency	FAILED_DEPENDENCY	424
TooManyRequest	TOO_MANY_REQUEST	429
InternalServerError	INTERNAL_SERVER_ERROR	500
NotImplemented	NOT_IMPLEMENTED	501
BadGateway	BAD_GATEWAY	502
ServiceUnavailable	SERVICE_UNAVAILABLE	503
GatewayTimeout	GATEWAY_TIMEOUT	504
HttpVersionNotSupported	HTTP_VERSION_NOT_SUPPORTED	505
InsufficientStorage	INSUFFICIENT_STORAGE	507

Asynchronous Actions

Suppose that we are at a food court and place an order to eat something at a kiosk, we are given a token and a bill. Later, when the order is ready, the kiosk flashes the token number, and upon noticing it, we collect the order.

This is similar to a request with an asynchronous response cycle, where the kiosk acts like the server, the order acts similar to a request, and the token as a promise, which gets resolved when the order is ready.

Most operations are better handled asynchronously. This is also mostly preferred since it does not block server resources until the operation is completed.

Play Action is a helper object, which extends the `ActionBuilder` trait. The apply method of the `ActionBuilder` trait implements the `Action` trait, which we saw earlier. Let's take a look at the relevant code from the `ActionBuilder` trait:

```
trait ActionBuilder[+R[_]] extends ActionFunction[Request, R] {
  self =>

  final def apply[A](bodyParser: BodyParser[A])(block: R[A] =>
    Result): Action[A] = async(bodyParser) { req: R[A] =>
    Future.successful(block(req))
  }

  final def async[A](bodyParser: BodyParser[A])(block: R[A] =>
    Future[Result]): Action[A] = composeAction(new Action[A] {
    def parser = composeParser(bodyParser)
    def apply(request: Request[A]) = try {
      invokeBlock(request, block)
    } catch {
      // NotImplementedError is not caught by NonFatal, wrap it
      case e: NotImplementedError => throw new RuntimeException(e)
      // LinkageError is similarly harmless in Play Framework, since
automatic reloading could easily trigger it
      case e: LinkageError => throw new RuntimeException(e)
    }
    override def executionContext =
      ActionBuilder.this.executionContext
  })

  ...


}
```

Notice that the `apply` method itself calls the `async` method internally. The `async` method expects us to define the Action, which results in `Future[Result]`, thereby aiding us to write non-blocking code.

We will use the same method to define an asynchronous Action. Assume that we need to fetch the requested file from a remote client, consolidate/analyze the data, and then send the results. Since we do not know the size of the file and the status of network connectivity with a remote client, it is better to handle the Action asynchronously. The action will be defined in this way:

```
def getReport(fileName:String ) = Action.async {
    Future {
      val file:File = new File(fileName)
```

```
   if (file.exists()) {
     val info = file.lastModified()
     Ok(s"lastModified on ${new Date(info)}")
   }
   else
     NoContent
  }
}
```

After fetching the file, if it is empty, we send a response with a status code of 204, else we continue with the processing and send the processed data as a part of the result.

We may come across an instance, as we saw in the previous example, get report, that we do not wish to wait longer than 10 seconds for the remote client to fetch the file. In this case, we'll need to modify the Action definition in this way:

```
def getReport(fileName: String) = Action.async {

  val mayBeFile = Future {

    new File(fileName)

  }

  val timeout = play.api.libs.concurrent.Promise.timeout("Past
    max time", 10, TimeUnit.SECONDS)

  Future.firstCompletedOf(Seq(mayBeFile, timeout)).map {
    case f: File =>

      if (f.exists()) {

        val info = f.lastModified()

        Ok(s"lastModified on ${new Date(info)}")

      }

      else

        NoContent

    case t: String => InternalServerError(t)

  }

}
```

So, if the remote client doesn't respond with the requested file in 10 seconds, we will get a response with status code 500 and the content as the message we set for the timeout, Past max time.

Content negotiation

According to HTTP:

> *Content negotiation is the process of selecting the best representation for a given response when there are multiple representations available.*

It can either be server-driven or agent-driven or a combination of both, which is called transparent negotiation. Play provides support for server-driven negotiations. This is handled by the rendering trait and is extended by the controller trait. The controller trait is the one where the controller objects in a Play app extend.

Let's look at the Rendering trait:

```
trait Rendering {

  object render {

    //Tries to render the most acceptable result according to the
request's Accept header value.
    def apply(f: PartialFunction[MediaRange, Result])(implicit
      request: RequestHeader): Result = {
      def _render(ms: Seq[MediaRange]): Result = ms match {
        case Nil => NotAcceptable
        case Seq(m, ms @ _*) =>
          f.applyOrElse(m, (m: MediaRange) => _render(ms))
      }

      // "If no Accept header field is present, then it is assumed
that the client accepts all media types."
      val result =
        if (request.acceptedTypes.isEmpty) _render(Seq(new
          MediaRange("*", "*", Nil, None, Nil)))
        else _render(request.acceptedTypes)
      result.withHeaders(VARY -> ACCEPT)
    }

    /**Tries to render the most acceptable result according to the
request's Accept header value.
      * This function can be used if you want to do asynchronous
processing in your render function.
```

```
  */
  def async(f: PartialFunction[MediaRange, Future[Result]])(implicit
  request: RequestHeader): Future[Result] = {
    def _render(ms: Seq[MediaRange]): Future[Result] = ms match {
      case Nil => Future.successful(NotAcceptable)
      case Seq(m, ms @ _*) =>
        f.applyOrElse(m, (m: MediaRange) => _render(ms))
    }

    // "If no Accept header field is present, then it is assumed
that the client accepts all media types."
    val result =
      if (request.acceptedTypes.isEmpty) _render(Seq(new
        MediaRange("*", "*", Nil, None, Nil)))
      else _render(request.acceptedTypes)
    result.map(_.withHeaders(VARY -> ACCEPT))
    }
  }
}
```

The `_render` method defined in the `apply` method calls the partial `f` function on the accept headers in the request. If `f` is not defined for the any of the accept headers, a response with status code 406 is forwarded. If it's not, the result of `f` for the first accept header for which `f` is defined, is returned.

Since the controller extends the rendering trait, we can use the render object within our Action definition. For example, we might have an Action, which gets the configuration in JSON and XML after reading it from a file with an XML format, depending on the accept headers in the request. Let's see how this is done:

```
def getConfig = Action {
    implicit request =>
      val xmlResponse: Node = <metadata>
        <company>TinySensors</company>
        <batch>md2907</batch>
      </metadata>

      val jsonResponse = Json.obj("metadata" -> Json.arr(
        Json.obj("company" -> "TinySensors"),
        Json.obj("batch" -> "md2907"))
      )
      render {
        case Accepts.Xml() => Ok(xmlResponse)
        case Accepts.Json() => Ok(jsonResponse)
      }
    }
```

In this snippet, `Accepts.Xml()` and `Accepts.Json()` are Play's helper methods that check to see if the request accepts the response of the `application/xml` and `application/json` types, respectively. There are currently four predefined accepts and these are tabulated here:

Request accept helper	Accept header value
XML	`application/xml`
JSON	`application/json`
HTML	`text/html`
JavaScript	`text/javascript`

This is facilitated by the `RequestExtractors` trait and the `AcceptExtractors` trait. `RequestExtractors` is also extended by the controller trait. Let's look at the extractor traits here:

```
trait RequestExtractors extends AcceptExtractors {

  //Convenient extractor allowing to apply two extractors.
  object & {
    def unapply(request: RequestHeader): Option[(RequestHeader,
      RequestHeader)] = Some((request, request))
  }

}


//Define a set of extractors allowing to pattern match on the Accept
HTTP header of a request
trait AcceptExtractors {

  //Common extractors to check if a request accepts JSON, Html, etc.
  object Accepts {
    import play.api.http.MimeTypes
    val Json = Accepting(MimeTypes.JSON)
    val Html = Accepting(MimeTypes.HTML)
    val Xml = Accepting(MimeTypes.XML)
    val JavaScript = Accepting(MimeTypes.JAVASCRIPT)
  }

}


//Convenient class to generate extractors checking if a given mime
type matches the Accept header of a request.
```

```
case class Accepting(val mimeType: String) {
  def unapply(request: RequestHeader): Boolean =
    request.accepts(mimeType)
  def unapply(mediaRange: play.api.http.MediaRange): Boolean =
    mediaRange.accepts(mimeType)
}
```

From this code, all that we need to define a custom accepts is the value we would expect the request's accept header to have. For example, to define a helper for `image/png`, we use this code:

```
val AcceptsPNG = Accepting("image/png")
```

We also notice that `RequestExtractors` has an `&` object, and we can use this when we wish to send the same response to multiple accept types. So, in the `getConfig` method shown in the preceding code, if the same response response is sent for `application/json` and `text/javascript`, we will modify it as follows:

```
def fooBar = Action {
    implicit request =>
      val xmlResponse: Node = <metadata>
        <company>TinySensors</company>
        <batch>md2907</batch>
      </metadata>

      val jsonResponse = Json.obj("metadata" -> Json.arr(
        Json.obj("company" -> "TinySensors"),
        Json.obj("batch" -> "md2907"))
      )

      render {
        case Accepts.Xml() => Ok(xmlResponse)
        case Accepts.Json() & Accepts.JavaScript() =>
          Ok(jsonResponse)
      }
    }
```

The `render` object can be used similarly when defining an asynchronous Action.

Filters

In most applications, we need to perform the same operation for all requests. We might be required to add a few fields to all the responses at a later stage, after we have already defined all the actions needed for our application.

So, in this case, will we have to update all the Actions?

No. This is where the filter API comes to our rescue. We don't need to modify how we define our Actions to solve the problem. All we need to do is define a filter and use it.

Let's see how we can define our filter:

```scala
import org.joda.time.DateTime
import org.joda.time.format.DateTimeFormat
import play.api.mvc._
import play.api.http.HeaderNames._
import play.api.libs.concurrent.Execution.Implicits.defaultContext

object HeadersFilter {
  val noCache = Filter {
    (nextFilter, rh) =>
      nextFilter(rh) map {
        case result: Result => addNoCacheHeaders(result)
      }
  }

  private def addNoCacheHeaders(result: Result): Result = {
    result.withHeaders(PRAGMA -> "no-cache",
      CACHE_CONTROL -> "no-cache, no-store, must-revalidate, max-
        age=0",
      EXPIRES -> serverTime)
  }

  private def serverTime = {
    val now = new DateTime()
    val dateFormat = DateTimeFormat.forPattern(
      "EEE, dd MMM yyyy HH:mm:ss z")
    dateFormat.print(now)
  }
}
```

The `HeadersFilter.noCache` filter adds all the headers to a response, which are required to disable caching in browsers. PRAGMA, CACHE_CONTROL, and EXPIRES are constants provided by `play.api.http.HeaderNames`.

Now, to use this filter, we would need to update the global settings for the application.

The global settings for any Play-based application can be configured using a global object. This is an object that's defined with the name `Global` and is placed in the app directory. We will find out more about global settings in *Chapter 7, Playing with Globals*.

There are two ways of defining how the filter should be used. These are:

1. Extending the `WithFilters` class instead of `GlobalSettings` for the global object.

2. Invoking the filter manually in the global object.

    An example of using `WithFilters` is:

    ```
    object Global extends WithFilters(HeadersFilter.noCache) {
      // ...
    }
    ```

    Now, let's see how this can be done manually:

    ```
    object Global extends GlobalSettings {
      override def doFilter(action: EssentialAction):
        EssentialAction = HeadersFilter.noCache(action)
    }
    ```

    In Play, a filter is defined similar to Action—there is a filter trait, which extends `EssentialFilter` and a helper filter object. The helper filter is defined as:

    ```
    object Filter {
      def apply(filter: (RequestHeader => Future[Result],
        RequestHeader) => Future[Result]): Filter = new Filter {
        def apply(f: RequestHeader => Future[Result])(rh:
          RequestHeader): Future[Result] = filter(f, rh)
      }
    }
    ```

    In this code snippet, the `apply` method calls a new filter, which is the filter trait.

    Multiple filters can be applied for a single application. If `WithFilters` is used, they are applied in the specified order. If they are set manually, we can use the filters object used internally by the apply method of the `WithFilters` class. The `Filters` object is defined as follows:

    ```
    object Filters {
      def apply(h: EssentialAction, filters: EssentialFilter*) = h
        match {
    ```

```
      case a: EssentialAction => FilterChain(a,
        filters.toList)
      case h => h
    }
  }
```

FilterChain is another helper object used to compose EssentialAction from a combination of EssentialAction and multiple EssentialFilters:

```
object FilterChain {
  def apply[A](action: EssentialAction, filters:
List[EssentialFilter]): EssentialAction = new EssentialAction {
    def apply(rh: RequestHeader): Iteratee[Array[Byte], Result] =
{
      val chain = filters.reverse.foldLeft(action) { (a, i) =>
        i(a) }
      chain(rh)
    }
  }
}
```

3. Filters are recommended when some operation is to be performed indiscriminately for all routes. Play provides a filter module, which has a GzipFilter, SecurityHeadersFilter, and CSRFFilter.

Action composition

Defining an Action for a request is merely the act of using the Action helper object, which is defined as follows:

```
object Action extends ActionBuilder[Request] {
  def invokeBlock[A](request: Request[A], block: (Request[A]) =>
    Future[Result]) = block(request)
}
```

The code which we write within an action block goes on to be the invokeBlock method. This method is inherited from ActionBuilder. This is a trait that provides helper methods to generate an Action. All the different ways in which we define an Action, such as async, synchronous, with or without specifying a parser, and so on are declared in ActionBuilder.

We can also define our custom Actions by extending ActionBuilder and defining a custom invoke block.

The need for an Action composition

Let's take a case study. A lot of applications these days keep track of requests, such as the IP address of the machine it was instigated from, the time it was received, or even the whole request as is. It would be a crime to add the same code in almost every Action defined for such an application.

Now, assume that we need to persist a request using a `persistReq` method every time it is encountered for a specific module: the administrator user, for example. Then, in this case, we could define a custom Action to be used only within this module. Let's see how we can define a custom Action to persist a request before processing it:

```
import play.api.mvc._
import scala.concurrent.Future

object TrackAction extends ActionBuilder[Request] {
  override protected def invokeBlock[A](request: Request[A], block:
(Request[A]) => Future[Result]) = {
    persistReq(request)
    block(request)
  }

  private def persistReq[A](request: Request[A]) = {
    ...
  }
}
```

Within our application, we could use it similar to the default Action:

```
def viewAdminProfile(id: Long) = TrackAction {
  request =>
    ...
}

def updateAdminProfile(id: Long) = TrackAction(parse.json) {
  request =>
    ...
}
```

Another way to define a custom Action is by extending the Action trait. So, we can also define `TrackAction` as follows:

```
case class TrackAction[A](action: Action[A]) extends Action[A] {

  def apply(request: Request[A]): Future[Result] = {
```

```
        persistReq(request)
        action(request)
    }

    private def persistReq(request: Request[A]) = {
        ...
    }

    lazy val parser = action.parser
}
```

Its usage would be something similar to this:

```
def viewAdminProfile(id: Long) = TrackAction {
    Action {request =>
        ...
    }
}

def updateAdminProfile(id: Long) = TrackAction {
    Action(parse.json) {      request =>
        ...
    }
}
```

Notice that we need to wrap the Action definition again within the action object. We could remove this additional overhead of wrapping an action object every time by defining ActionBuilder, which uses the composeAction method:

```
object TrackingAction extends ActionBuilder[Request] {
    def invokeBlock[A](request: Request[A], block: (Request[A]) =>
Future[Result]) = {
        block(request)
    }
    override def composeAction[A](action: Action[A]) = new
TrackAction(action)
}
```

Now, the usage will be:

```
def viewAdminProfile(id: Long) = TrackingAction {
    request =>
        ...
}

def updateAdminProfile(id: Long) = TrackingAction(parse.json) {
```

```
request =>
    ...
}
```

Differentiating between Action composition and filters

Action composition is an Action that extends `EssentialAction` and returns a result. It is more suitable when we need to perform an operation on a few routes or Actions only. Action composition is more powerful than a filter and is more apt at handling specific concerns, such as authentication.

It provides support to read, modify, and even block a request. There is also a provision to define Actions for custom request types.

Customized requests

First, let's see how to define custom requests. We can also define custom requests using the `WrappedRequest` class. This is defined as follows:

```
class WrappedRequest[A](request: Request[A]) extends Request[A] {
    def id = request.id
    def tags = request.tags
    def body = request.body
    def headers = request.headers
    def queryString = request.queryString
    def path = request.path
    def uri = request.uri
    def method = request.method
    def version = request.version
    def remoteAddress = request.remoteAddress
    def secure = request.secure
}
```

Suppose we wish to pass the time at which a request was received with every request, we could define this as:

```
class TimedRequest[A](val time: DateTime, request: Request[A])
  extends WrappedRequest[A](request)
```

Now, let's see how we can manipulate the incoming requests and transform them into `TimedRequest`:

```
def timedAction[A](action: Action[A]) =
  Action.async(action.parser) {
```

```
    request =>
      val time = new DateTime()
      val newRequest = new AppRequest(time, request)
      action(newRequest)
}
```

Therefore, the `timedAction` Action can be used within controllers in this way:

```
def getUserList = timedAction {
    Action {
      request =>
        val users= User.getAll
        Ok(Json.toJson(users))
    }
}
```

Now, suppose we wish to block all the requests from certain browsers; it can be done in this way:

```
def timedAction[A](action: Action[A]) =
  Action.async(action.parser) {
  request =>
    val time = new DateTime()
    val newRequest = new AppRequest[A](time, request)
    request.headers.get(USER_AGENT).collect {
      case agent if isCompatibleBrowser(agent) =>
        action(newRequest)
      }.getOrElse{
      Future.successful(Ok(views.html.main()))
    }
}
```

Here, the `isCompatibleBrowser` method checks if the browser is supported.

We can also manipulate the response; let's add the duration it took to process the request in the response headers:

```
def timedAction[A](action: Action[A]) =
  Action.async(action.parser) {
   request =>
    val time = new DateTime()
    val newRequest = new AppRequest(time, request)
    action(newRequest).map(_.withHeaders("processTime" -> new
      DateTime().minus(time.getMillis).getMillis.toString()))
}
```

Now, let's see how we define an Action for a custom request. You may wonder why we need a custom request. Take the example where our application has a facility for the users to use e-mail, chat, block, upload, share, and so on. In this case, we could tie these so that we can have a user object as part of the request internally.

The need for a user object

Our REST API only sends `userId`, which is a number. For all these operations, we need the user's `emailId`, `userName`, and profile picture, if any. Let's define `UserRequest` in the following way:

```
class UserRequest[A](val user: User, request: Request[A]) extends
    WrappedRequest[A](request)
```

Now, let's define an Action, which uses this request:

```
def UserAction(userId: Long) = new ActionBuilder[UserRequest] {
   def invokeBlock[A](request: Request[A], block:
       (UserRequest[A]) => Future[Result]) = {
      User.findById(userId).map { user:User =>
         block(new UserRequest(user, request))
      } getOrElse {
         Future.successful(Redirect(views.html.login))
      }
   }
}
```

So, in our Action, we find the user corresponding to the given `userId`, else we redirect to the login page.

Here, we can see how to use `UserAction`:

```
def initiateChat(userId:Long,chatWith:Long) = UserRequest{
    request=>
      val status:Boolean =
        ChatClient.initiate(request.user,chatWith)
       if(status){
        Ok
      }else{
         Unauthorized
      }
}
```

The chat client initiates a method and sends a message to the user with `userId`. `chatWith` that a user, whose profile is `request.user`, wants to chat. It returns `true` if the other user agrees, else it returns `false`.

Troubleshooting

Here are the scenarios you might come across where you may need to troubleshoot:

1. Coming across an error during compilation: you cannot find any HTTP request header here.

    You get this error even after you have defined the Action using a `RequestHeader`.

    Most of the methods used in Play that deal with requests, expect an implicit `RequestHeader`. This convention has been followed in order to keep the code simple. For example, let's look at the controller trait here:

```
trait Controller extends Results with BodyParsers with
HttpProtocol with Status with HeaderNames with ContentTypes with
RequestExtractors with Rendering {

  //Provides an empty `Action` implementation: the result is a
standard 'Not implemented yet' result page.
  val TODO = Action {
    NotImplemented[play.api.templates.Html](views.html.
defaultpages.todo())
  }

  //Retrieves the session implicitly from the request.
  implicit def session(implicit request: RequestHeader) =
    request.session

  //Retrieve the flash scope implicitly from the request.
  implicit def flash(implicit request: RequestHeader) =
    request.flash

  implicit def lang(implicit request: RequestHeader) = {
    play.api.Play.maybeApplication.map { implicit app =>
      val maybeLangFromCookie =
        request.cookies.get(Play.langCookieName).flatMap(c
        => Lang.get(c.value))
        maybeLangFromCookie.getOrElse(play.api.i18n.Lang.
        preferred(request.acceptLanguages))
    }.getOrElse(request.acceptLanguages.headOption.getOrElse(play.
api.i18n.Lang.defaultLang))
  }
}
```

Notice that the `session`, `flash`, and `lang` methods accept an implicit parameter, such as a request, which is `RequestHeader`. It is in such cases that we need to mark the request header in our Action definition as implicit. Generally, it's safer to mark all the request headers as implicit in a Play application. So, to fix this error, we would need to modify our `Action` definition as follows:

```
def foo = Action {
    implicit request =>

    ...
}
```

2. The request body for my GET request is not parsed. You may wonder why. The GET request is not expected to have a request body. Though the HTTP specification is not clear on this, in general practice, browsers do not forward the request body. Play body parser checks to see if the request is allowed to have a request body, that is, if the request is not a GET request, before parsing it.

   It is better to avoid a request body in your GET and DELETE requests. If you need to add a request body to these requests, maybe you should redesign the REST API for your application.

3. You're not able to use the Play filters: `GzipFilter`, `SecurityHeadersFilter`, or `CSRFFilter`. You get an error: the object `filters` is not a member of package play, in line import `play.filters`.

   Filters is a separate module and needs to be included explicitly. You should add it the `build.sbt` file as the `libraryDependencies += filters`, and then reload the project.

4. Coming across a compilation error when using Future: if you cannot find an implicit `ExecutionContext`, either require one for yourself or import `ExecutionContext.Implicits.global`. Why should this be done, though?

   Future requires an `ExecutionContext`, which defines the thread pool where threads will be allotted for an operation. Hence, you might get a compilation error when no `ExecutionContext` is available for Future. Refer to the *Scala docs Futures* (`http://docs.scala-lang.org/overviews/core/futures.html`) section for more on this.

5. Coming across a runtime error while using the JSON parser:
   `JsResultException`:

   ```
   JsResultException(errors:List((,List(ValidationError(error.
     expected.jsstring,WrappedArray())))))]
   ```

This generally happens when the field being extracted from JSON is not present in the request body. This could be because there is a typo, for example, instead of emailId, and you might be sending an e-mail. You could use the asOpt method instead of as. For example:

```
val emailId = (body\"emailId"). asOpt[String]
```

Then you could throw an error with a human-friendly message if that or any field is missing. Alternatively, you could pass default values using getOrElse.

Summary

In this chapter, we saw how to define and extend the key components of a controller. We saw how to define an application-specific Action with default parsers and results, as well as with custom parsers and results. In addition to this, we also saw how to manage application-specific concerns using filters and ActionComposition. In the process, we saw how to define a custom request.

3
Building Routes

In this chapter, we will be covering the following topics:

- Defining the services supported by an application
- The flow of requests received
- Configuring routes
- Handling assets

Introduction to Play routes

All the supported routes are specified within a single file: routes (by default). This makes it all the easier to figure out which one would be ideal.

The routes file is compiled and if any errors occur, the compilation fails.

However, the routes file is not a Scala object. So how does the compiler know what to do with the routes file? To find this out, let's perform the following steps:

1. Let's create a project that displays a *Hello, World!* page. Now, define the index.scala.html home page as follows:

```
<!DOCTYPE html>
<html>
    <head>
        <title>Home</title>
    </head>
    <body>
        <h1>Hello, World!</h1>
    </body>
</html>
```

2. We will use this in our controller in this way:

```
package controllers

import play.api.mvc._
object AppController extends Controller {

  def index = Action {
    Ok(views.html.index())
  }

}
```

3. All we need to view our page is an entry in the `routes` file:

```
# Home page
GET              /                        controllers.AppController.index
```

4. Now compile the project. You will notice that a `routes_routing.scala` file is now available in the `HelloWorld/target/scala-2.10/src_managed/main` directory. The contents of the file will be similar to the following code snippet:

```
import play.core._
import play.core.Router._
import play.core.j._

import play.api.mvc._


import Router.queryString

object Routes extends Router.Routes {

private var _prefix = "/"

def setPrefix(prefix: String) {
  _prefix = prefix
  List[(String,Routes)]().foreach {
    case (p, router) => router.setPrefix(prefix +
      (if(prefix.endsWith("/")) "" else "/") + p)
  }
```

```scala
}

def prefix = _prefix

lazy val defaultPrefix = { if(Routes.prefix.endsWith("/"))
  "" else "/" }



// @LINE:5
private[this] lazy val controllers_AppController_index0 =
  Route("GET", PathPattern(List(StaticPart
  (Routes.prefix))))

def documentation = List((("""GET""", prefix,"""controllers.
AppController.index""")).foldLeft
  (List.empty[(String,String,String)]) { (s,e) =>
  e.asInstanceOf[Any] match {
  case r @ (_,_,_) => s :+
    r.asInstanceOf[(String,String,String)]
  case l => s ++
    l.asInstanceOf[List[(String,String,String)]]
}}



def routes:PartialFunction[RequestHeader,Handler] = {

// @LINE:5
case controllers_AppController_index0(params) => {
   call {
        invokeHandler(controllers.AppController.index,
          HandlerDef(this, "controllers.AppController",
          "index", Nil,"GET", """ Routes
 This file defines all application routes (Higher priority routes
first)
 ~~~~
 Home page""", Routes.prefix + """"""))
   }
}


}


}
```

So, Play generates Scala code from the routes file. A routes partial function is created using the routes file. The call method takes a function that returns a handler and defines the parameters to be passed to it. It is defined to handle 0 to 21 parameters.

The invokeHandler method is defined as follows:

```
def invokeHandler[T](call: => T, handler: HandlerDef)(implicit d:
    HandlerInvoker[T]): Handler = {
        d.call(call, handler) match {
            case javaAction: play.core.j.JavaAction => new
                play.core.j.JavaAction with RequestTaggingHandler {
                def invocation = javaAction.invocation
                val annotations = javaAction.annotations
                val parser = javaAction.annotations.parser
                def tagRequest(rh: RequestHeader) = doTagRequest(rh,
                    handler)
            }
            case action: EssentialAction => new EssentialAction with
                RequestTaggingHandler {
                def apply(rh: RequestHeader) = action(rh)
                def tagRequest(rh: RequestHeader) = doTagRequest(rh,
                    handler)
            }
            case ws @ WebSocket(f) => {
                WebSocket[ws.FRAMES_TYPE](rh => f(doTagRequest(rh,
                    handler)))(ws.frameFormatter)
            }
            case handler => handler
        }
```

The result from d.call(call and handler) is matched to the predefined play.core.j.JavaAction, EssentialAction, and WebSocket types (all of which extend the handler trait) and their result is returned.

HandlerDef is a class, which is defined as follows:

```
case class HandlerDef(ref: AnyRef, routerPackage: String,
    controller: String, method: String, parameterTypes:
    Seq[Class[_]], verb: String, comments: String, path: String)
```

Automatic generation of routes_routing.scala

Let's have a look at how the `routes_routing.scala` file is generated.

Play utilizes the features provided by **Simple Build Tool (SBT)** to add a source generation task. A source generation task should generate sources in a subdirectory of `sourceManaged` and return a sequence of the files generated.

The SBT documentation can be found at `http://www.scala-sbt.org/0.13.2/docs/Howto/generatefiles.html`.

The usage can be seen in `PlaySettings.scala`, as follows:

```
sourceGenerators in Compile <+= (state, confDirectory,
    sourceManaged in Compile, routesImport, generateReverseRouter,
    generateRefReverseRouter, namespaceReverseRouter) map {
    (s, cd, sm, ri, grr, grrr, nrr) => RouteFiles(s, Seq(cd), sm,
    ri, grr, grrr, nrr)
},
```

`RouteFiles` is defined in the `PlaySourceGenerators` trait, which handles the Scala code generation for routes and views. Yes, even views are transformed to Scala code. For example, an `index.template.scala` file is available for the `HelloWorld` project at `HelloWorld/target/scala-2.10/src_managed/main/views/html`.

The definition for `RouteFiles` calls the `RoutesCompiler.compile` method and then returns the file paths where the source will be generated. The `compile` method parses the file using `RouteFileParser` and then generates the Scala code using the `generateRouter` method.

Reverse routing

Play provides a feature to make HTTP calls using Scala methods. For every route defined, an equivalent Scala method is generated in the `routes_ReverseRouting.scala` file. This is very convenient when making a request from within our Scala code, for example, within views such as the following:

```
@(tasks: List[Task], taskForm: Form[String])

@import helper._

@main("Task Tracker") {

    <h2>Task Tracker</h2>

    <div>
```

```
@form(routes.TaskController.newTask) {

    @taskForm.globalError.map { error =>
        <p class="error">
            @error.message
        </p>
    }
    <form>
        <input type="text" name="taskName" placeholder="Add a
            new Task" required>

        <input type="submit" value="Add">
    </form>
}
</div>
<div>
    <ul>
    @tasks.map { task =>
        <li>
            @form(routes.TaskController.deleteTask(task.id)) {
                @task.name <input type="submit"
                    value="Remove">
            }
        </li>
    }
    </ul>
</div>

}
```

The content of the `routes_reverseRouting.scala` file would be similar to the following:

```
import Routes.{prefix => _prefix, defaultPrefix => _defaultPrefix}
import play.core._
import play.core.Router._
import play.core.j._

import play.api.mvc._


import Router.queryString


// @LINE:5
```

```
package controllers {

// @LINE:5
class ReverseAppController {


// @LINE:5
def index(): Call = {
   Call("GET", _prefix)
}



}

}



// @LINE:5
package controllers.javascript {

// @LINE:5
class ReverseAppController {


// @LINE:5
def index : JavascriptReverseRoute = JavascriptReverseRoute(
  "controllers.AppController.index",
   """
     function() {
     return _wA({method:"GET", url:"""" + _prefix + """"})
     }
   """
)



}

}



// @LINE:5
```

```
package controllers.ref {


// @LINE:5
class ReverseAppController {


// @LINE:5
def index(): play.api.mvc.HandlerRef[_] = new
  play.api.mvc.HandlerRef(
    controllers.AppController.index(), HandlerDef(this,
      "controllers.AppController", "index", Seq(), "GET", """
      Routes
 This file defines all application routes (Higher priority routes
first)
 ~~~~
 Home page""", _prefix + """""")
)



}


}
```

The reverse routes return a call. A call describes an HTTP request and can be used to create links or fill and redirect data. It is defined as follows:

```
case class Call(method: String, url: String) extends play.mvc.Call {

    //Transform this call to an absolute URL.
    def absoluteURL(secure: Boolean = false)(implicit request:
      RequestHeader) = {
      "http" + (if (secure) "s" else "") + "://" + request.host +
        this.url
    }


    // Transform this call to an WebSocket URL.
    def webSocketURL(secure: Boolean = false)(implicit request:
      RequestHeader) = {
      "ws" + (if (secure) "s" else "") + "://" + request.host +
        this.url
    }


    override def toString = url

  }
```

JavaScript reverse routing

In `routes_reverseRouting.scala`, there is also a method that returns `JavascriptReverseRoute`. We could use this in our JavaScript code when we wish to send a request. Prior to this, however, we would need to define a JavaScript router. We could do this by defining an action and then adding a route for it, as shown in this example:

```
def javascriptRoutes = Action { implicit request =>
  Ok(
    Routes.javascriptRouter("jsRouter")(
      routes.javascript.index
    )
  ).as("text/javascript")
}
```

Then, we could include it in the routes file in this way:

```
GET /javascriptRoutes   controllers.AppController.javascriptRoutes
```

Next, we could refer to it in our views as follows:

```
<script type="text/javascript"
  src="@routes.AppController.javascriptRoutes"></script>
```

Once this is done, in our JavaScript scripts we could use the router to send requests to the server, as follows:

```
jsRouter.controllers.AppController.index.ajax({
  success: function(data) {
    console.log("redirect successful");
  },
  error:function(e){
    console.log("something terrible happened" + e);
  }
});
```

Assets

Any web application would require a style sheet or some other resources such as images, scripts, and so in. In a non-Play application, we would refer to these by figuring out the relative location of the file. For example, suppose that our application has a `webapp` folder with `index.html`, where we need to add a `homePage.css` stylesheet, which is located at `webapp/styles`. Now, the reference in `index.html` would be something similar to the following:

```
<link rel="stylesheet" href="styles/homePage.css" />
```

Such relative paths can get very confusing and, at times, difficult to manage. In a Play application, the resources are placed in the public directory and can be accessed using a request. It is suggested that you split the public directory into three subdirectories for images, CSS style sheets, and JavaScript files for consistency, as shown in the following figure:

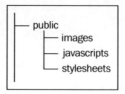

In addition to this, Play provides an asset controller by default to support requests, which can access resources (assets). In most Play applications, a route for assets is also available in the routes file, as shown here:

```
GET            /assets/*file          controllers.Assets.at(path="/
public", file)
```

This route gives access to resources, such as style sheets, scripts, and so on. A file is expected to be the remainder of the path after `/public`, which is required to access it. For example, to get the `homePage.css` style sheet, we would send a GET request to `/assets/stylesheets/homePage.css`. The path preceded by `/assets/` is considered to be the path for the file.

In views, we would need to use a `routes` helper. So, if we wish to add a style sheet in one of our views, we would refer to it as follows:

```
<link rel="stylesheet"
  href="@routes.Assets.at("stylesheets/homePage.css")" />
```

Similarly, we will refer to a JavaScript script as follows:

```
<script src="@routes.Assets.at("javascripts/slider.js")"
  type="text/javascript"></script>
```

It is also possible to specify a separate path for images, style sheets, or scripts so that the request paths are shorter, as shown here:

```
GET            /styles/*file          controllers.Assets.at(path="/
public/styles", file)
```

```
GET            /images/*file          controllers.Assets.at(path="/
public/images", file)
```

The Action at is defined as follows:

```
def at(path: String, file: String, aggressiveCaching: Boolean =
  false): Action[AnyContent] = Action.async {
  implicit request =>

    import Implicits.trampoline
    val pendingResult: Future[Result] = for {
      Some(name) <- Future.successful(resourceNameAt(path,
        file))
      (assetInfo, gzipRequested) <- assetInfoForRequest(request,
        name)
    } yield {
      val stream = assetInfo.url(gzipRequested).openStream()
      Try(stream.available -> Enumerator.fromStream(stream)
        (Implicits.defaultExecutionContext)).map {
        case (length, resourceData) =>
          maybeNotModified(request, assetInfo,
            aggressiveCaching).getOrElse {
            cacheableResult(
              assetInfo,
              aggressiveCaching,
              result(file, length, assetInfo.mimeType,
                resourceData, gzipRequested,
                assetInfo.gzipUrl.isDefined)
            )
          }
      }.getOrElse(NotFound)
    }

    pendingResult.recover {
      case e: InvalidUriEncodingException =>
        Logger.debug(s"Invalid URI encoding for $file at $path",
          e)
        BadRequest
      case e: Throwable =>
        Logger.debug(s"Unforseen error for $file at $path", e)
        NotFound
    }
}
```

If a *gzipped* version of a file is available, the asset controller will serve that instead. A gzipped version refers to the version of the file that was obtained by compressing the file using gzip. It adds the .gz extension to the filename.

As well as the resource, `AssetController` adds the `etag` header.

The `etag` acronym is used for an entity tag. This is a unique identifier for the resource being requested, and is generally a hash of the resource or of its last modified timestamp.

Client-side libraries

Views in most applications rely on third-party libraries. In Play, we could define dependencies located in such libraries using **webJars** and **npm**.

Play extracts the assets from the WebJar dependencies as well as from npm packages into the `lib` directory within the public assets. We can refer to these when defining an asset with a dependency on the files present there. For example, if our view depends on `d3.js`, then we use the following:

```
<script src="@routes.Assets.at("lib/d3/d3.v3.min.js")"
  charset="utf-8"></script>
```

WebJars are JARs of libraries used for the client-side development of a web application.

npm is an acronym for node packaged modules. It is the package manager for Node.js. It allows developers to install registered modules through the command line.

To use a WebJar, we would need to define our project's dependency on it just as in any other module, as shown here:

```
libraryDependencies+="org.webjars" % "d3js" % "3.4.6-1"
```

To include npm packages, we would need to place the `package.json` file in a project root. The `package.json` file would be similar to this:

```
{
  "name": "myApp",
  "version": "1.0.0",
  "dependencies": {
  },
  "devDependencies": {
    "grunt": "~0.4.1",
    "grunt-contrib-concat": "~0.1.3",
    "grunt-contrib-cssmin": "~0.5.0",
    "grunt-contrib-clean": "~0.4.0",
    "grunt-contrib-less": "~0.7.0"
  },
```

```
    "engines": {
      "node": ">=0.8.0"
    }
  }
}
```

Configuring route definitions

Play supports both static and dynamic request paths. If a request path cannot be matched to any of the defined routes, an `Action not found` error is thrown at runtime, which is rendered using the `devNotFound.scala.html` default template.

Dynamic paths

Dynamic paths are those that can be used for multiple requests and they may or may not result in a similar response. For example, the default assets path is a path used to serve resources:

```
GET           /assets/*file          controllers.Assets.at(path="/
public", file)
```

The * symbol indicates that anything following `/assets/` until a space is found is the value of the `file` variable.

Let's look at another way to make the path dynamic when we need to add one or more variables. For example, to get a user's details by `userId` we use the following code:

```
GET           /api/user/:userId     controllers.UserController.
getUser(userId)
```

By default, all the variables that occur in a path are of the `String` type. If a conversion is required, the type should be mentioned explicitly. So, if the `getUser` method takes a long parameter, we would just need to specify it in this way:

```
GET           /api/user/:userId     controllers.UserController.
getUser(userId:Long)
```

Using the":" prefix for `userId` means that the `userId` variable is exactly one URI part. The assets path uses *any suffix indicator* as the relative file path, which is required to access any file.

It is not necessary that a path should end with a variable; for example, `/api/user/:userId/album` can be used as a valid path to fetch all the albums stored by a user.

Multiple variables can also be used in the same path. Supposing we wished to fetch a specific album, we could use `/api/user/:userId/album/:albumId`.

The maximum number of variables we can specify in a path is 21, since this is the maximum that the `call` method used in `routes_routing.scala` is defined to handle. Also, the request path becomes complicated and ends up with too many variables. In general, keeping the number of such parameters to less than five is a good practice.

Play also supports using regular expressions to match the variables. For example, assume that we want to restrict a string variable to consisting of only letters, such as a region code; in this case, our route can be defined as follows:

```
GET             /api/region/$regionId<[a-zA-Z]{2}>/user
controllers.UserController.getUserByRegion(regionId)
```

Notice that when we specify a regular expression for the variable in the route, it is prefixed with a `$` symbol instead of the `:` symbol while defining the route.

The preceding route definition restricts the request by a regular expression. For example:

- `/api/region/IN/user` is a valid path
- `/api/region/CABT/user` and `/api/region/99/user` are invalid

The order of preference to a route is defined by its position in the `routes` file. The router returns the first matching route for a given path. If the same request type and route are mapped for two different actions, the compiler does not throw an error or warning. Some IDEs indicate when duplicate route definitions occur, but it is completely the developer's responsibility to ensure that such cases do not occur.

This table summarizes the different ways of defining a dynamic path:

Sr.no.	Purpose	Special characters	Example usage(s)
1	URI path separator is part of the variable	*	`/assets/*file`

2	Single or multiple variables	:	`/api/user/:userId`
			`/api/user/:userId/album`
			`/api/user/:userId/album/:albumId`

3	Regular expression pattern for variables	$	`/api/region/$regionId<[a-zA-Z]{2}>/user`

Static paths

Static request paths are fixed and constant. They cannot support arguments in the request path. All the data required for such requests should be sent through request parameters or request bodies. For example, the actions used for signing in or signing out are given as follows:

```
GET             /login              controllers.Application.login
```

So does Play search for specific characters to identify the kind of path?

Yes, the special characters are used by `RoutesFileParser` to recognize whether a path is static or dynamic. The paths are defined as follows:

```
def singleComponentPathPart: Parser[DynamicPart] = (":" ~>
  identifier) ^^ {
  case name => DynamicPart(name, """[^/]+""", encode = true)
}


def multipleComponentsPathPart: Parser[DynamicPart] = ("*" ~>
  identifier) ^^ {
  case name => DynamicPart(name, """.+""", encode = false)
}


def regexComponentPathPart: Parser[DynamicPart] = "$" ~>
  identifier ~ ("<" ~> (not(">") ~> """[^\s]""".r +) <~ ">" ^^
  { case c => c.mkString }) ^^ {
  case name ~ regex => DynamicPart(name, regex, encode =
    false)
}


def staticPathPart: Parser[StaticPart] = (not(":") ~> not("*") ~>
not("$") ~> """[^\s]""".r +) ^^ {
  case chars => StaticPart(chars.mkString)
}
```

In the methods used to identify a path, the `~>`, `not`, and `^^` methods are from `scala.util.parsing.combinator.{Parser, RegexParsers}`. `DynamicPart` and `StaticPart` are defined with the intention of capturing the parts of a URL, so that it's simpler to pass values to a corresponding action. They are defined as follows:

```
trait PathPart

case class DynamicPart(name: String, constraint: String, encode:
Boolean) extends PathPart with Positional {
  override def toString = """DynamicPart("""" + name + "\",
    \"\"\"" + constraint + "\"\"\"," + encode + ")" //"
```

```
    }

    case class StaticPart(value: String) extends PathPart {
      override def toString = """StaticPart("""" + value + """")"""
    }

    case class PathPattern(parts: Seq[PathPart]) {
      def has(key: String): Boolean = parts.exists {
        case DynamicPart(name, _, _) if name == key => true
        case _ => false
      }

      override def toString = parts.map {
        case DynamicPart(name, constraint, encode) => "$" + name + "<"
          + constraint + ">"
        case StaticPart(path) => path
      }.mkString

    }
```

Configuring request parameters

Many applications use additional parameters along with RESTful HTTP GET requests to obtain required information. Play supports configuring these request parameters as well.

Supposing we have a request to search users by their name, we could define this as follows:

```
GET           /api/search/user      controllers.UserController.
search(name)
```

Therefore, we wouldn't need to get the parameters from the request in the action. We could let Play handle acquiring the parameters from the request and passing them to the action.

What do we do when the request parameters are optional? For example, what happens if we allow a search of users by their name where lastName is optional.

We can specify Option as the type for this request parameter. Therefore, the route definition would be similar to the following:

```
GET           /api/search/user      controllers.UserController.
search(firstName:String,
  lastName:Option[String])
```

In addition to this, we can also specify the default value, if any, for request parameters. Suppose we had a limit parameter for the search request as well. In this case, if we wish to set the default value as 10, the route definition would be as follows:

```
GET            /api/search/user      controllers.UserController.
search(firstName:String,
   lastName:Option[String], limit:Int ?= 10)
```

Troubleshooting

The application works as expected but when the code is added to one or more base packages, the reverse routing doesn't work.

The routes are compiled, so when you make changes to the controllers, the project should be recompiled. In this case, run the `clean` command and then compile the project. It is better to see whether the generated routing files reflect the changes made. If not, delete the target directory and compile the project.

Summary

In this chapter, we saw what an essential role routing plays in a Play application. As well as this, we saw the various default methods that Play provides to simplify the process of routing, in the form of assets, reverse routing, and so on.

In the next chapter, we will see how to define views in a Play application and also uncover how it works. As well as from the templating mechanism, the internals of building and using forms and internationalization will be covered in detail.

4
Exploring Views

Views are an essential part of an application, or, in cases where interaction is minimal, they are the means to show what an application is capable of. They have the power to increase the number of end users or discourage them completely. Views that enhance the user experience are always preferred over those that are as complicated as a maze, through which the user struggles to perform a simple task. They act as a deciding factor in an application's success.

In this chapter, we will cover the following topics:

- Building views using Twirl
- Generating Form
- Internationalization
- Templating Internals (covers basics of how Twirl works)

Diving into Scala templates

A **Twirl** template is composed of parameters and content. The following figure shows the components of a login page template called `login.scala.html`:

The parameters must be declared first since they are used as the parameters of the `apply` method of the generated template object. For example, for the `main.scala.html` template, shown in the preceding code, the `apply` method will be:

```
def apply/*1.2*/(title:
    String)(content:play.api.twirl.Html)
    :play.api.templates.HtmlFormat.Appendable = {...}
```

The template content can be HTML as well as Scala code.

For example, let's look at some `defaultpages` (accessible through the object `views.html.defaultpages`) bundled along with Play. The default view for this action is not implemented; `todo.scala.html` has no template parameters and has plain HTML for its content. It is defined as follows:

```
<!DOCTYPE html>
<html>
  <head>
    <title>TODO</title>
    <link rel="shortcut icon"
      href="data:image/png;base64,iVBORw..">
    <style>
    ...
    </style>

  </head>
  <body>
    <h1>TODO</h1>

    <p id="detail">
      Action not implemented yet.
    </p>

  </body>
</html>
```

Similarly, the default view for unauthorized, `unauthorized.scala.html`, is also a static page.

Now, let's check how the view for action not found in development mode,
devNotFound.scala.html is defined:

```
@(request:play.api.mvc.RequestHeader,
  router:Option[play.core.Router.Routes])

<!DOCTYPE html>
<html>
  <head>
    <title>Action not found</title>
    <link rel="shortcut icon"
      href="data:image/png;base64,iVBORw..">
  </head>
  <body>
    <h1>Action not found</h1>

    <p id="detail">
      For request '@request'
    </p>

    @router match {

      case Some(routes) => {

        <h2>
          These routes have been tried, in this order:
        </h2>

          <div>
@routes.documentation.zipWithIndex.map { r =>
  <pre><span class="line">@(r._2 + 1)</span><span
    class="route"><span class="verb">@r._1._1</span><span
    class="path">@r._1._2</span><span
    class="call">@r._1._3</span></span></pre>
}
          </div>

      }

      case None => {
        <h2>
          No router defined.
```

```
        </h2>
    }


    }


    </body>
</html>
```

In the template snippets, the style component has been excluded to focus on the Scala code used.

If there is a route file defined, then it lists all the available routes in a preformatted block. The methods defined for the type of the template parameter can be called even within the template. For example, if `books: Seq[String]` is one of the parameters, we can call `@books.length` or `@books.map{...}`, and so on, within the template.

Additionally, a Twirl template can be used within another template. This allows us to have reusable chunks of views. For example, supposing we have a main template, which is used by all other views, the application's theme (which includes the header, footer, basic layout, and so on) can be updated by tweaking the main template. Consider a template `main.scala.html`, defined as follows:

```
@(title: String)(content: play.twirl.api.Html)

<!DOCTYPE html>

<html>
    <head>
      <title>@title</title>
    </head>
    <body>
    <header>brand name</header>
    @content
    <footer>Copyright 2013</footer>
    </body>
</html>
```

Reusing this template will be as simple as the following:

```
@main("locate us"){
   <div>
     company address
   </div>
}
```

Another example is defining *widgets* as templates. These widget templates can then be used in multiple views of the application. Similarly, we can also define code blocks within our templates.

Building a view

Let's build a view, which is commonly found in today's web applications. A view where the user is asked to select the account they want to log in with, such as Google, Facebook, and so on, is given a list of providers with the condition that, by default, the first provider should be selected.

Consider that in the list of supported third-party authentications, `otherAuth` is passed as a template parameter. The type of `otherAuth` is `Seq[ThirdPartyAuth]`, where `ThirdyPartyAuth` is a case class defined to represent any third-party authentication API.

So, this is completed as follows:

```
<div>
    <p>
       Please select the account you wish to use

       @for(auth <- otherAuth) {
         <input type="radio" name="account" value="@auth.id">
           @auth.name
    <br/>
         }
    </p>
</div>
```

In this snippet, we used `for` to iterate through all the supported third-party authentications. In the templates, we can use two Scala functions, `for` and `if`, in addition to those defined within the template and the ones defined on the basis of the type of template parameters.

Now, the only important part remaining is to set the default value. We can achieve this by using one of the utility methods provided by Twirl the `defining` method. Let's create a variable to check whether the provider is the first one or not. We can then have different markups for the two possibilities. If we modify our code to accommodate this, we will get this code:

```
<div>
    <p>
```

```
        Please select the account you wish to use

        @for(auth <- otherAuth) {
            @defining(auth.id == otherAuth.head.id) { isChecked =>
                @if(isChecked) {
                    <input type="radio" name="account"
                      value="@auth.id" checked="checked">
                      @auth.name
                    } else {
                    <input type="radio" name="account"
                      value="@auth.id"> @auth.name
                    }
            }
        <br/>
        }
    </p>
</div>
```

Generating forms

Forms are important in situations where the application requires input from users, for example, in the case of registration, login, search, and so on.

Play provides helpers to generate a form and wrapper classes to translate the form data into a Scala object.

Now, we'll build a user registration form using the form helper provided by Play:

```
@helper.form(action = routes.Application.newUser) {
  <label>Email Id
  <input type="email" name="email" tabindex="1"
    required="required">
      </label>

      <label>Password
        <input type="password" name="password" tabindex="2"
          required="required">
      </label>

      <input type="submit" value="Register" type="button">
}
```

Here, `@helper.form` is a template provided by Play, which is defined as follows:

```
@(action: play.api.mvc.Call, args: (Symbol,String)*)(body: =>
  Html)

<form action="@action.url" method="@action.method"
  @toHtmlArgs(args.toMap)>
  @body
</form>
```

We can also provide other parameters for the `form` element as a tuple of `Symbol` and `String`. The `Symbol` component will become the parameter and its corresponding `String` component will be set as its value in the following way:

```
@helper.form(action = routes.Application.newUser, 'enctype ->
  "multipart/form-data")
```

The resulting HTML will now be as follows:

```
<form action="/register" method="POST" enctype="multipart/form-
  data">...</form>
```

This is possible due to the `toHtmlArgs` helper method, defined as follows:

```
def toHtmlArgs(args: Map[Symbol, Any]) =
  play.twirl.api.Html(args.map({
  case (s, None) => s.name
  case (s, v) => s.name + "=\"" +
    play.twirl.api.HtmlFormat.escape(v.toString).body + "\""
}).mkString(" "))
```

Now, when we try to register a user, the request body within the action will be:

```
AnyContentAsFormUrlEncoded(Map(email ->
  ArrayBuffer(testUser@app.com), password ->
  ArrayBuffer(password)))
```

If the `enctype` parameter is specified, and the request is parsed as `multipartformdata`, the request body will be as follows:

```
MultipartFormData(Map(password -> List(password), email ->
  List(testUser@app.com)),List(),List(),List())
```

Instead of defining custom methods to take a map so that it results in a corresponding model, we can use the `play.api.data.Form` form data helper object.

The form object aids in the following:

- Mapping form data to user-defined models (such as case classes) or tuples
- Validating the data entered to see if it meets the required constraints. This can be done for the all of the fields collectively, independently for each field, or both.
- Filling in default values.

We might need to have the form data translated into credentials; in this case, the class is defined as follows:

```
case class Credentials(loginId: String, password: String)
```

We can update the registration view to use the form object in the following way:

```
@import models.Credentials

@(registerForm: Form[Credentials])(implicit flash: Flash)

@main("Register") {
    <div id="signup" class="form">
    @helper.form(action = routes.Application.newUser, 'enctype ->
      "multipart/form-data") {
        <hr/>
        <div>

            <label>Email Id
              <input type="email" name="loginId" tabindex="1"
                required="required">
            </label>

            <label>Password
              <input type="password" name="password" tabindex="2"
                required="required">
            </label>

        </div>
        <input type="submit" value="Register">
        <hr/>
          Existing User?<a
            href="@routes.Application.login()">Login</a>
        <hr/>
    }
    </div>
}
```

Now we define a form that creates a credentials object from a form with the `loginId` and `password` field:

```
val signupForm = Form(
    mapping(
      "loginId" -> email,
      "password" -> nonEmptyText
    )(Credentials.apply)(Credentials.unapply)
```

We now define the following actions:

```
    def register = Action {
      implicit request =>
        Ok(views.html.register(signupForm)).withNewSession
    }

    def newUser = Action(parse.multipartFormData) {
      implicit request =>
        signupForm.bindFromRequest().fold(
          formWithErrors =>
            BadRequest(views.html.register(formWithErrors)),
          credentials => Ok
        )
    }
```

The `register` and `newUser` methods are mapped to GET /register and POST / register, respectively. We pass the form in the view so that when there are errors in form validation, they are shown in the view along with the form fields. We will see this in detail in the following section.

Let us now see how this works. When we fill the form and submit, the call goes to the `newUser` action. The `signupForm` is a form and is defined as follows:

```
case class Form[T](mapping: Mapping[T], data: Map[String, String],
    errors: Seq[FormError], value: Option[T]) { … }
```

We used the constructor, which is defined in its companion object:

```
def apply[T](mapping: Mapping[T]): Form[T] = Form(mapping,
  Map.empty, Nil, None)
```

The `mapping` method can accept a maximum of 18 arguments. Forms can also be defined using the `tuple` method, which will in turn call the `mapping` method:

```
def tuple[A1, A2](a1: (String, Mapping[A1]), a2: (String,
  Mapping[A2])): Mapping[(A1, A2)] = mapping(a1, a2)((a1: A1, a2:
  A2) => (a1, a2))((t: (A1, A2)) => Some(t))
```

Using this, instead of mapping for `signupForm`, you will get this code:

```
val signupForm = Form(
    tuple(
        "loginId" -> email,
        "password" -> nonEmptyText
    )
)
```

 The terms `email` and `nonEmptyText`, which we used while defining the form using mapping as well as the tuple, are predefined constraints and are also defined in the `Form` object. The following section discusses them in detail.

When defining forms that have a single field, we can use the `single` method since the tuple is not defined for a single field, as shown here:

```
def single[A1](a1: (String, Mapping[A1])): Mapping[(A1)] =
    mapping(a1)((a1: A1) => (a1))((t: (A1)) => Some(t))
```

The method called in our action is `signupForm.bindRequestFrom`. The `bindRequestFrom` method takes an implicit request and fills the form with the form data in the request.

Once we have filled the form, we need to check if it has any errors or not. This is where the `fold` method comes in handy, as defined here:

```
def fold[R](hasErrors: Form[T] => R, success: T => R): R = value
    match {
    case Some(v) if errors.isEmpty => success(v)
    case _ => hasErrors(this)
}
```

The variable errors and value are from the form constructor. The type of error is `Seq[FormError]`, whereas that of the value is `Option[T]`.

We then map the result from `fold` to `BadRequest(formWithErrors)` if the form has errors. If it doesn't, we can continue with the handled data submitted through the form.

Adding constraints on data

It is a common requirement to restrict the form data entered by users with one rule or another. For example, checking to ensure that the name field data does not contain digits, the age is less than 18 years, if an expired card is being used to complete the transaction, and so on. Play provides default constraints, which can be used to validate the field data. Using these constraints, we can define a form easily as well as restrict the field data in some ways, as shown here:

```
mapping(
    "userName" -> nonEmptyText,
    "emailId" -> email,
    "password" -> nonEmptyText(minLength=8,maxLength=15)
    )
```

The default constraints can be broadly classified into two categories: the ones that define a simple `Mapping[T]`, and the ones that consume `Mapping[T]` and result in `Mapping[KT]`, as shown here:

```
mapping(
    "userName" -> nonEmptyText,
    "interests" -> list(nonEmptyText)
    )
```

In this example, `Mapping[String]` is transformed into `Mapping[List[String]]`.

There are two other constraints that do not fall into either category. They are `ignored` and `checked`.

The `ignored` constraint can be used when we do need mapping from the user data for that field. For example, fields such as login time or logout time should be filled in by an application and not the user. We could use `mapping` in this way:

```
mapping(
    "loginId" -> email,
    "password" -> nonEmptyText,
    "loginTime" -> ignored(System.currentTimeMillis())
    )
```

The `checked` constraint can be used when we need to ensure that a particular checkbox has been selected by the user. For example, accepting terms and conditions of the organization, and so on, in `signupForm`:

```
mapping(
    "loginId" -> email,
    "password" -> nonEmptyText,
    "agree" -> checked("agreeTerms")
    )
```

The constraints of the first category are listed in this table:

Constraint	Results in	Additional properties and their default values (if any)
text	Mapping[String]	minLength: 0, maxLength: Int.MaxValue
nonEmptyText	Mapping[String]	minLength: 0, maxLength: Int.MaxValue
number	Mapping[Int]	min: Int.MinValue, max: Int.MaxValue, strict: false
longNumber	Mapping[Long]	min: Long.MinValue, max: Long.MaxValue, strict: false
bigDecimal	Mapping[BigDecimal]	precision, scale
date	Mapping[java.util.Date]	pattern, timeZone: java.util.TimeZone.getDefault
sqlDate	Mapping[java.sql.Date]	pattern, timeZone: java.util.TimeZone.getDefault
jodaDate	Mapping[org.joda.time.DateTime]	pattern, timeZone: org.joda.time.DateTimeZone.getDefault
jodaLocalDate	Mapping[org.joda.time.LocalDate]	pattern
email	Mapping[String]	
boolean	Mapping[Boolean]	

This table lists the constraints included in the second category:

Constraint	Results in	Required parameters and their type
optional	Mapping[Option[A]]	mapping: Mapping[A]
default	Mapping[A]	mapping: Mapping[A], value: A
list	Mapping[List[A]]	mapping: Mapping[A]

Constraint	Results in	Required parameters and their type
seq	Mapping[Seq[A]]	mapping: Mapping[A]
set	Mapping[Seq[A]]	mapping: Mapping[A]

In addition to these field constraints, we can also define ad hoc and/or custom constraints on a field using the `verifying` method.

An instance might arise where an application lets users choose their `userName`, which can only consist of numbers and alphabet. To ensure that this rule is not broken, we can define an ad hoc constraint:

```
mapping(
"userName" ->  nonEmptyText(minLength=5) verifying pattern("""[A-
   Za-z0-9]*""".r, error = "only digits and alphabet are allowed in
   userName"
)
```

Or, we can define a custom constraint using the `Constraint` case class:

```
val validUserName = """[A-Za-z0-9]*""".r
val userNameCheckConstraint: Constraint[String] =
  Constraint("contraints.userName")({
    text =>
      val error = text match {
        case validUserName() => Nil
        case _ => Seq(ValidationError("only digits and alphabet
          are allowed in userName"))
      }
      if (error.isEmpty) Valid else Invalid(error)
  })

val userNameCheck: Mapping[String] = nonEmptyText(minLength =
  5).verifying(passwordCheckConstraint)
```

We can use this in a form definition:

```
mapping(
"userName" ->  userNameCheck
)
```

Note that `nonEmpty`, `minLength`, `maxLength`, `min`, `max`, `pattern`, and `email` are predefined constraints. They are defined in the `play.api.data.validation` trait. The available constraints can be used as references when defining custom constraints.

Handling errors

What happens when one or more constraints has been broken in the form that has been submitted? The `bindFromRequest` method creates a form with errors, which we earlier referred to as `formWithErrors`.

For each violated constraint, an error is saved. An error is represented by `FormError`, defined as follows:

```
case class FormError(key: String, messages: Seq[String], args:
    Seq[Any] = Nil)
```

The `key` is the name of the field where a constraint was broken, `message` is its corresponding error message and `args` are the arguments, if any, used in the message. In the case of constraints defined in multiple fields, the key is an empty string and such errors are termed `globalErrors`.

The errors in a form for a specific field can be accessed through the `errors` method, defined as:

```
def errors(key: String): Seq[FormError] = errors.filter(_.key == key)
```

For example:

```
registerForm.errors("userName")
```

Alternatively, to access only the first error, we can use the `error` method instead. It is defined as follows:

```
def error(key: String): Option[FormError] = errors.find(_.key ==
    key)
```

Now, how do we access `globalErrors` (that is, an error from a constraint defined in multiple fields together)?

We can use the form's `globalErrors` method, which is defined as follows:

```
def globalErrors: Seq[FormError] = errors.filter(_.key.isEmpty)
```

If we want just the first `globalError` method, we can use the `globalError` method. It is defined as follows:

```
def globalError: Option[FormError] = globalErrors.headOption
```

When we use the form-field helpers, field-specific errors are mapped to the field and displayed if they're present. However, if we are not using the form helpers, we will need to display the errors, as shown here:

```
<label>Password
  <input type="password" name="password" tabindex="2"
    required="required">
</label>
@registerForm.errors("password").map{ er => <p>@er.message</p>}
```

The `globalErrors` method needs to be added to the view explicitly, as shown here:

```
@registerForm.globalErrors.map{ er => <p>@er.message</p>}
```

Form-field helpers

In the previous example, we used the HTML code for the `form` fields, but we can also do this using the `form` field helpers provided by Play. We can update our view, `@import models.Credentials`, as shown here:

```
@(registerForm: Form[Credentials])(implicit flash: Flash)

@main("Register") {
  @helper.form(action = routes.Application.newUser, 'enctype ->
    "multipart/form-data") {
    @registerForm.globalErrors.map { error =>
      <p class="error">
        @error.message
      </p>
    }

    @helper.inputText(registerForm("loginId"), 'tabindex -> "1",
      '_label -> "Email ID",
    'type -> "email", 'required -> "required", '_help -> "A valid
      email Id")

    @helper.inputPassword(registerForm("password"), 'tabindex ->
      "2",
    'required -> "required", '_help -> "preferable min.length=8")

    <input type="submit" value="Register">
    <hr/>
    Existing User?<a href="@routes.Application.login()">Login</a>
    }
}
```

Let's see how this works. The helper `inputText` is a view defined as follows:

```
@(field: play.api.data.Field, args: (Symbol,Any)*)(implicit
   handler: FieldConstructor, lang: play.api.i18n.Lang)

@inputType = @{
   args.toMap.get('type).map(_.toString).getOrElse("text") }

@input(field, args.filter(_._1 != 'type):_*) { (id, name, value,
   htmlArgs) =>
      <input type="@inputType" id="@id" name="@name" value="@value"
        @toHtmlArgs(htmlArgs)/>
}
```

It uses the input helper internally, which is also a view and can be defined as follows:

```
@(field: play.api.data.Field, args: (Symbol, Any)* )(inputDef:
   (String, String, Option[String], Map[Symbol,Any]) =>
   Html)(implicit handler: FieldConstructor, lang:
   play.api.i18n.Lang)

@id = @{ args.toMap.get('id).map(_.toString).getOrElse(field.id) }

@handler(
      FieldElements(
          id,
          field,
          inputDef(id, field.name, field.value, args.filter(arg =>
             !arg._1.name.startsWith("_") && arg._1 != 'id).toMap),
          args.toMap,
          lang
      )
)
```

Both the `form` field helpers use an implicit `FieldConstructor`. This field constructor is responsible for the HTML rendered. By default, `defaultFieldConstructor` is forwarded. It is defined as follows:

```
@(elements: FieldElements)

<dl class="@elements.args.get('_class) @if(elements.hasErrors)
   {error}" id="@elements.args.get('_id).getOrElse(elements.id +
   "_field")">
      @if(elements.hasName) {
      <dt>@elements.name(elements.lang)</dt>
      } else {
```

```
    <dt><label for="@elements.id">@elements.label
      (elements.lang)</label></dt>
    }
    <dd>@elements.input</dd>
    @elements.errors(elements.lang).map { error =>
        <dd class="error">@error</dd>
    }
    @elements.infos(elements.lang).map { info =>
        <dd class="info">@info</dd>
    }
</dl>
```

So, if we wish to change the layouts for our `form` fields, we can define a custom `FieldConstructor` and pass it to the `form` field helpers, as shown here:

```
@input(contactForm("name"), '_label -> "Name", '_class -> "form-
  group", '_size -> "100") { (id, name, value, htmlArgs) =>
  <input class="form-control" type="text" id="@id" name="@name"
  value="@value" @toHtmlArgs(htmlArgs)/>
}
```

This section attempts to explain how the form helper works; for more examples, refer to the Play Framework documentation at `http://www.playframework.com/documentation/2.3.x/ScalaForms`.

Internationalization

Due to the wide reach of the Internet, it is now possible to communicate and interact with people from diverse locations. An application that communicates with users in one specific language restricts its user base through the use of only that language. Internationalization and localization can be used to cater to user groups from various regions by removing barriers that arise due to the use of a particular language only.

Now, let's build a simple view, which allows us to ask a question. The `views/index.scala.html` view file will be similar to the following:

```
@(enquiryForm: Form[(String, Option[String], String)])

@import helper._

@main("Enquiry") {

    <div>
```

```
            <h2>Have a question? Ask Us</h2>

            @form(routes.AppController.enquire) {

                @enquiryForm.globalError.map { error =>
                    <p>
                        @error.message
                    </p>
                }

                <label for="emailId">Your email address
                    <input type="email" id="emailId" name="emailId"
                        required>
                </label>

                <label for="userName">Your name
                    <input type="text" class="form-control"
                        id="userName" name="userName">
                </label>

                <label for="question">Your question
                    <textarea rows="4" id="question"
                        name="question"></textarea>
                </label>

                <br/>
                <button type="submit">Ask</button>
            }
        </div>
}
```

Here, `AppController` is a controller and is defined as follows:

```
package controllers

import play.api.mvc._
import play.api.data.Form
import play.api.data.Forms._


object AppController extends Controller {

  val enquiryForm = Form(
    tuple(
      "emailId" -> email,
```

```
      "userName" -> optional(text),
      "question" -> nonEmptyText)
  )

  def index = Action {
    implicit request =>
      Redirect(routes.AppController.askUs)
  }

  def askUs = Action {
    implicit request =>
      Ok(views.html.index(enquiryForm))
  }

  def enquire = Action {
    implicit request =>
      enquiryForm.bindFromRequest.fold(
        errors => BadRequest(views.html.index(errors)),
        query => {
          println(query.toString)
          Redirect(routes.AppController.askUs)
        }
      )
  }

}
```

The main template views/main.scala.html is defined as follows:

```
@(title: String)(content: Html)
<!DOCTYPE html>

<html>
    <head>
        <title>@title</title>
    </head>
    <body>
    @content
    </body>
</html>
```

The routes for the application are defined as follows:

```
# Home page
GET          /                      controllers.AppController.index


# Other
GET          /ask                   controllers.AppController.askUs
POST         /enquire               controllers.AppController.enquire
```

Now when we start the application, with the help of a little bit of styling (CSS styles), our view looks similar to this:

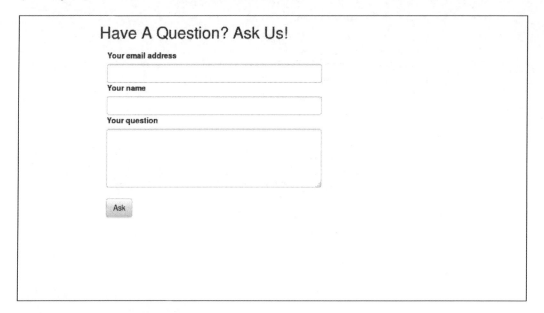

Supporting views in multiple languages

We might want our application to be available in both English and French. Therefore, having different views for different languages is a bad idea. This would mean that every time the support for a language is included, we would need to define all the views in our application in this particular language as well. Using Play's *i18n* support, supporting another language can be as simple as adding a file that contains translations.

Firstly, we will need to specify the languages supported by our application in
`conf/application.conf`. Notice that this is commented code in the default
`conf/application.conf`, which indicates the following:

```
# The application languages
# ~~~~~
# application.langs="en"
```

The format in which the language should be specified is its ISO 639-2 code,
optionally followed by an ISO 3166-1 alpha-2 country code. You can include
French as well, as shown here:

```
application.langs="en,fr"
```

In Play, the translations required for content to be rendered in a particular language
are called messages. For each language, we need to provide a `conf/messages.`
`lang-code` file. If we wish to have common content, we should define it in `conf/`
`messages`; this can be quite useful for names, branding, and so on.

Let's create a `messages` file for English called `conf/messages.en`:

```
enquiry.title = Enquiry
enquiry.askUs=Have A Question? Ask Us!
enquiry.user.email=Your email address
enquiry.user.name=Your name
enquiry.question=Your question
enquiry.submit=Ask
```

Now we need to update our view to use these messages, in the form of
`@(enquiryForm: Form[(String, Option[String], String)])`
`(implicit lang: Lang)`:

```
@import helper._

@main(Messages("enquiry.title")) {

    <div>
        <h2>@Messages("enquiry.askUs")</h2>

        @form(routes.AppController.enquire) {

            @enquiryForm.globalError.map { error =>
                <p>
                    @error.message
                </p>
```

```
            }

            <label for="emailId">@Messages("enquiry.user.email")
                <input type="email" id="emailId" name="emailId"
                    required>
            </label>

            <label for="userName">@Messages("enquiry.user.name")
                <input type="text" class="form-control"
                    id="userName" name="userName">
            </label>

            <label for="question">@Messages("enquiry.question")
                <textarea rows="4" id="question"
                    name="question"></textarea>
            </label>

            <br/>
            <button type="submit">@Messages
                ("enquiry.submit")</button>
        }
    </div>
}
```

Now, let's add the French messages file, `conf/messages.fr`:

```
enquiry.title = Demande de renseignements
enquiry.askUs = Vous avez une question? Demandez-nous!
enquiry.user.email = Votre adresse e-mail
enquiry.user.name = Votre nom
enquiry.question = Votre question
enquiry.submit = Demandez
```

Change your browser settings so that you have French (fr) enabled as the primary language and run the application. You should be able to see the enquiry view in French:

We can also use the messages within the Scala code after importing `play.api.i18n`:

```
val title = Messages("enquiry.title")
```

Understanding internationalization

When we use `Messages` (word) in our code, it calls the `apply` method of the `play.api.i18n.Messages` object. The `apply` method is defined as follows:

```
def apply(key: String, args: Any*)(implicit lang: Lang): String = {
    Play.maybeApplication.flatMap { app =>
      app.plugin[MessagesPlugin].map(_.api.translate(key,
        args)).getOrElse(throw new Exception("this plugin was not
        registered or disabled"))
    }.getOrElse(noMatch(key, args))
}
```

Play has an internal plugin called the `MessagesPlugin`, defined as follows:

```
class MessagesPlugin(app: Application) extends Plugin {

  import scala.collection.JavaConverters._

  import scalax.file._
  import scalax.io.JavaConverters._

  private def loadMessages(file: String): Map[String, String] = {
```

```
app.classloader.getResources(file).asScala.toList.reverse.map
  { messageFile =>
  new Messages.MessagesParser(messageFile.asInput,
    messageFile.toString).parse.map { message =>
    message.key -> message.pattern
  }.toMap
}.foldLeft(Map.empty[String, String]) { _ ++ _ }
}


private lazy val messages = {
  MessagesApi {
    Lang.availables(app).map(_.code).map { lang =>
      (lang, loadMessages("messages." + lang))
    }.toMap + ("default" -> loadMessages("messages"))
  }
}


//The underlying internationalization API.
def api = messages


//Loads all configuration and message files defined in the
classpath.
override def onStart() {
  messages
}


}
```

This plugin is responsible for loading all the messages and generating a `MessagesApi`
object, which is later used to fetch the value of a message. So, when we refer to a
message, it's fetched from this instance of `MessagesApi`. `MessagesApi` and is defined
as follows:

```
case class MessagesApi(messages: Map[String, Map[String, String]]) {

  import java.text._

  //Translates a message.
  def translate(key: String, args: Seq[Any])(implicit lang: Lang):
    Option[String] = {
    val langsToTry: List[Lang] =
      List(lang, Lang(lang.language, ""), Lang("default", ""),
        Lang("default.play", ""))
    val pattern: Option[String] =
      langsToTry.foldLeft[Option[String]](None)((res, lang) =>
```

```
            res.orElse(messages.get(lang.code).flatMap(_.get(key))))
      pattern.map(pattern =>
        new MessageFormat(pattern,
          lang.toLocale).format(args.map
          (_.asInstanceOf[java.lang.Object]).toArray))
  }

  //Check if a message key is defined.
  def isDefinedAt(key: String)(implicit lang: Lang): Boolean = {
    val langsToTry: List[Lang] = List(lang, Lang(lang.language,
      ""), Lang("default", ""), Lang("default.play", ""))

    langsToTry.foldLeft[Boolean](false)({ (acc, lang) =>
      acc || messages.get(lang.code).map
        (_.isDefinedAt(key)).getOrElse(false)
    })
  }

}
```

 The implicit `lang` parameter is the key to get messages in the accepted language.

Scala templating in Play

Play supports the use of Scala code within views and also provides a couple of helper methods to ease the process of defining a view.

We've created different views till now. Let's see how they are actually rendered. Consider the view for the Task Tracker app we saw in *Chapter 1, Getting Started with Play.*

```
@(tasks: List[Task], taskForm: Form[String])

@import helper._

@main("Task Tracker") {

    <h2>Task Tracker</h2>

    <div>
```

```
@form(routes.TaskController.newTask) {

    @taskForm.globalError.map { error =>
        <p class="error">
            @error.message
        </p>
    }
    <form>
        <input type="text" name="taskName" placeholder="Add a
          new Task" required>

        <input type="submit" value="Add">
    </form>
}
</div>
<div>
    <ul>
    @tasks.map { task =>
        <li>
            @form(routes.TaskController.deleteTask(task.id)) {
                @task.name <input type="submit"
                  value="Remove">
            }
        </li>
    }
    </ul>
</div>

}
```

The view has Scala code along with HTML, so how is it rendered correctly?

Open the Task Tracker view in a browser without running the Play application. The browser renders the page as follows:

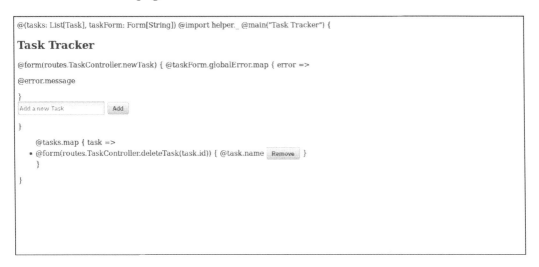

```
@(tasks: List[Task], taskForm: Form[String]) @import helper._ @main("Task Tracker") {

Task Tracker

@form(routes.TaskController.newTask) { @taskForm.globalError.map { error =>

@error.message

}
Add a new Task            Add

}

    @tasks.map { task =>
  • @form(routes.TaskController.deleteTask(task.id)) { @task.name  Remove  }
    }

}
```

Now have a look at how differently it is rendered when you run the Play application!

When a Play application is compiled, the route-related files (`routes_reverseRouting.scala` and `routes_routing.scala`, `controllers/routes.java`) and Scala views are generated. The routes-related files are generated through the **routes compiler**, while the Scala views are generated by the **template compiler**. The Scala template engine of Play has been extracted to facilitate its use in projects independent of Play. The Play Scala template engine is now available as Twirl. According to `https://github.com/spray/twirl`, the reason for choosing Twirl as the name is:

> As a replacement for the rather unwieldy name "Play framework Scala template engine" we were looking for something shorter with a bit of "punch" and liked Twirl as a reference to the template languages "magic" character @, which is sometimes also called "twirl".

Understanding the working of Twirl

Play's plugin is defined with a dependency on **SbtTwirl**; we can see this in the plugin definition:

```
object Play
  extends AutoPlugin
  with PlayExceptions
  with PlayReloader
  with PlayCommands
  with PlayRun
  with play.PlaySettings
  with PlayPositionMapper
  with PlaySourceGenerators {

  override def requires = SbtTwirl && SbtJsTask && SbtWebDriver

  val autoImport = play.PlayImport


  override def projectSettings =
    packageArchetype.java_server ++
      defaultSettings ++
      intellijCommandSettings ++
      Seq(testListeners += testListener) ++
      Seq(
        scalacOptions ++= Seq("-deprecation", "-unchecked", "-
          encoding", "utf8"),
        javacOptions in Compile ++= Seq("-encoding", "utf8", "-g")
      )
}
```

In addition to this, there are some SBT keys defined in `defaultSettings` using **TwirlKeys**. TwirlKeys exposes some keys, which can be used to customize Twirl as per our requirement. The keys that are exposed using TwirlKeys are:

- `twirlVersion`: This is the Twirl version used for twirl-api dependency (`SettingKey[String]`).

- `templateFormats`: This defines Twirl template formats (`SettingKey[Map[String, String]]`). The default formats available are `html`, `txt`, `xml`, and `js`.

- `templateImports`: This includes the extra imports used for twirl templates (`SettingKey[Seq[String]]`). By default, its value is an empty sequence.

- useOldParser: This uses the original Play template parser (SettingKey[Boolean]); the value is false by default.

- sourceEncoding: This includes the source encoding for template files and generated Scala files (TaskKey[String]). If no encoding is specified in Scala compiler options, it uses the UTF-8 encoding.

- compileTemplates: This compiles twirl templates into Scala source files (TaskKey[Seq[File]]).

To understand this task, let's see how twirlSettings are defined in the Twirl plugin:

```
def twirlSettings: Seq[Setting[_]] = Seq(
  includeFilter in compileTemplates := "*.scala.*",
  excludeFilter in compileTemplates := HiddenFileFilter,
  sourceDirectories in compileTemplates :=
    Seq(sourceDirectory.value / "twirl"),

  sources in compileTemplates <<= Defaults.collectFiles(
    sourceDirectories in compileTemplates,
    includeFilter in compileTemplates,
    excludeFilter in compileTemplates
  ),

  watchSources in Defaults.ConfigGlobal <++= sources in
    compileTemplates,

  target in compileTemplates := crossTarget.value / "twirl" /
    Defaults.nameForSrc(configuration.value.name),

  compileTemplates := compileTemplatesTask.value,

  sourceGenerators <+= compileTemplates,
  managedSourceDirectories <+= target in compileTemplates
)
```

The compileTemplates setting gets its value from compileTemplatesTask.value. The compileTemplatesTask in turn returns the result from the TemplateCompiler. compile method, as shown here:

```
def compileTemplatesTask = Def.task {
  TemplateCompiler.compile(
    (sourceDirectories in compileTemplates).value,
    (target in compileTemplates).value,
    templateFormats.value,
    templateImports.value,
    (includeFilter in compileTemplates).value,
```

```
        (excludeFilter in compileTemplates).value,
        Codec(sourceEncoding.value),
        useOldParser.value,
        streams.value.log
      )
    }


  ...

  }
```

`TemplateCompiler.compile` **is defined as follows:**

```
def compile(
    sourceDirectories: Seq[File],
    targetDirectory: File,
    templateFormats: Map[String, String],
    templateImports: Seq[String],
    includeFilter: FileFilter,
    excludeFilter: FileFilter,
    codec: Codec,
    useOldParser: Boolean,
    log: Logger) = {

    try {
      syncGenerated(targetDirectory, codec)
      val templates = collectTemplates(sourceDirectories,
        templateFormats, includeFilter, excludeFilter)
      for ((template, sourceDirectory, extension, format) <-
        templates) {
        val imports = formatImports(templateImports, extension)
        TwirlCompiler.compile(template, sourceDirectory,
          targetDirectory, format, imports, codec, inclusiveDot =
          false, useOldParser = useOldParser)
      }
      generatedFiles(targetDirectory).map(_.getAbsoluteFile)
    } catch handleError(log, codec)
  }
```

The `compile` method creates the `target/scala-scalaVersion/src_managed`
directory within the project if it does not already exist. If it exists, then it deletes
all the files that match the `"*.template.scala"` pattern through the `cleanUp`
method. After this, the `collectTemplates` method gets `Seq[(File, String,`
`TemplateType)]` by searching for files whose names match the `"*.scala.*"`
pattern and end with a supported extension.

Each object from the result of `collectTemplates` is then passed as an argument for `TwirlCompiler.compile`.

`TwirlCompiler.compile` is responsible for parsing and generating Scala templates and is defined as follows:

```
def compile(source: File, sourceDirectory: File,
  generatedDirectory: File,
formatterType: String, additionalImports: String = "",
  logRecompilation: (File, File) => Unit = (_, _) => ()) = {
    val resultType = formatterType + ".Appendable"
    val (templateName, generatedSource) = generatedFile(source,
      sourceDirectory, generatedDirectory)
    if (generatedSource.needRecompilation(additionalImports)) {
      logRecompilation(source, generatedSource.file)
      val generated = parseAndGenerateCode(templateName,
       Path(source).byteArray, source.getAbsolutePath, resultType,
       formatterType, additionalImports)

      Path(generatedSource.file).write(generated.toString)

      Some(generatedSource.file)
    } else {
      None
    }
  }
```

The `parseAndGenerateCode` method gets the parser and parses the file. The resulting parsed `Template` (internal object) is passed on to the `generateFinalCode` method. The `generateFinalCode` method is responsible for generating the code. Internally, it uses the `generateCode` method, which is defined as follows:

```
def generateCode(packageName: String, name: String, root:
  Template, resultType: String, formatterType: String,
  additionalImports: String) = {
  val extra = TemplateAsFunctionCompiler.getFunctionMapping(
    root.params.str,
    resultType)

  val generated = {
    Nil :+ """
package """ :+ packageName :+ """

import twirl.api._
```

```
import TemplateMagic._

    """ :+ additionalImports :+ """
/*""" :+ root.comment.map(_.msg).getOrElse("") :+ """*/
object """ :+ name :+ """ extends BaseScalaTemplate[""" :+
  resultType :+ """,Format[""" :+ resultType :+ """]](""" :+
  formatterType :+ """) with """ :+ extra._3 :+ """ {

    /*""" :+ root.comment.map(_.msg).getOrElse("") :+ """*/
    def apply""" :+ Source(root.params.str, root.params.pos) :+
      """:""" :+ resultType :+ """ = {
        _display_ {""" :+ templateCode(root, resultType) :+ """}
    }

  """ :+ extra._1 :+ """

  """ :+ extra._2 :+ """

  def ref: this.type = this

}"""
    }
    generated
}
```

The result from `parseAndGenerateCode` is written into its corresponding file.

Let's check out where we are going to use the file we generated!

Consider the view defined in *Chapter 1, Getting Started with Play*; the generated Scala template is similar to the following:

```
package views.html

import play.templates._
import play.templates.TemplateMagic._

import play.api.templates._
import play.api.templates.PlayMagic._
import models._
import controllers._
import play.api.i18n._
import play.api.mvc._
import play.api.data._
import views.html._
/**/
```

```
object index extends BaseScalaTemplate[play.api.templates.HtmlFormat.
Appendable,Format[play.api.templates.HtmlFormat.Appendable]](play.api.
templates.HtmlFormat) with play.api.templates.Template2[List[Task],For
m[String],play.api.templates.HtmlFormat.Appendable] {

    /**/
    def apply/*1.2*/(tasks: List[Task], taskForm:
      Form[String]):play.api.templates.HtmlFormat.Appendable = {
      _display_ {import helper._


Seq[Any](format.raw/*1.45*/("""


"""),format.raw/*4.1*/("""
"""),_display_(Seq[Any](/*5.2*/main("Task Tracker")/*5.22*/ {_display_
(Seq[Any](format.raw/*5.24*/("""

    <h2>Task Tracker</h2>

    <div>
    """),_display_(Seq[Any](/*10.6*/form
      (routes.TaskController.newTask)/*10.41*/
      {_display_(Seq[Any](format.raw/*10.43*/("""

        """),_display_(Seq[Any](/*12.10*/taskForm/*12.18*
          /.globalError.map/*12.34*/ { error
          =>_display_(Seq[Any](format.raw/*12.45*/("""
            <p class="error">
          """),_display_(Seq[Any](/*14.18*/error/*14.23*
            /.message)),format.raw/*14.31*/("""
            </p>
        """)))})),format.raw/*16.10*/("""
        <form>
            <input type="text" name="taskName" placeholder="Add a
              new Task" required>

            <input type="submit" value="Add">
        </form>
        """)))})),format.raw/*22.6*/("""
    </div>
    <div>
        <ul>
        """),_display_(Seq[Any](/*26.10*/tasks/*26.15*
          /.map/*26.19*/ { task
            =>_display_(Seq[Any](format.raw/*26.29*/("""
              <li>
```

```
        """),_display_(Seq[Any](/*28.18*/form
          (routes.TaskController.deleteTask(task.id))/*28.65*/
          {_display_(Seq[Any](format.raw/*28.67*/("""
        """),_display_(Seq[Any](/*29.22*/task/*29.26*/.name)
          ),format.raw/*29.31*/("""  <input type="submit"
        value="Remove">
                 """)))})),format.raw/*30.18*/("""
            </li>
        """)))})),format.raw/*32.10*/("""
            </ul>
        </div>


""")))}))))}
    }

    def render(tasks:List[Task],taskForm:Form[String]):
      play.api.templates.HtmlFormat.Appendable =
        apply(tasks,taskForm)

    def f:((List[Task],Form[String]) =>
      play.api.templates.HtmlFormat.Appendable) = (tasks,taskForm)
        => apply(tasks,taskForm)

    def ref: this.type = this

}
                /*
                    -- GENERATED --
                    DATE: Timestamp
                    SOURCE: /TaskTracker/app/views/index.scala.html
                    HASH: ff7c2a525ebc63755f098d4ef80a8c0147eb7778
                    MATRIX: 573->1|726->44|754->63|790->65|818-
>85|857->87|936->131|980->166|1020->168|1067->179|1084->187|1109-
>203|1158->214|1242->262|1256->267|1286->275|1345->302|1546->472|1626-
>516|1640->521|1653->525|1701->535|1772->570|1828->617|1868->619|1926-
>641|1939->645|1966->650|2053->705|2113->733
                    LINES: 19->1|23->1|25->4|26->5|26->5|26->5|31-
>10|31->10|31->10|33->12|33->12|33->12|33->12|35->14|35->14|35->14|37-
>16|43->22|47->26|47->26|47->26|47->26|49->28|49->28|49->28|50->29|50-
>29|50->29|51->30|53->32
                    -- GENERATED --
*/
```

So, when we refer to this view in a controller as `views.html.index(Task.all, taskForm)`, we are calling the `apply` method of the generated template object index.

Troubleshooting

Here are a few issues we can come across while using a Play view:

- The form is not submitted when you click on **Submit** and no errors are displayed using `globalErrors`.

  There may be a situation where a particular required field is missing or there is a typo in the name of the field. It will not be shown in `globalErrors` but if you attempt to display the error for an individual field, `error.required` will show up for the missing field.

- Do we need to use Twirl templates for the application's views?

  No, Play does not force developers to use Twirl templates for the views. They are free to design the views in whichever way they find easy or comfortable. For example, this can be done by using Handlebars, Google Closure templates, and so on.

- Does this affect the performance of the application in any way?

  No, unless there are no performance flaws in your view definitions, plugging it in a Play application will not affect the performance. There are projects that use the Play server for their native Android and iOS apps.

- Are there any other templating libraries supported by Play?

  No, but there some Play plugins which aid in using other templating mechanisms or libraries that are available. Since they are developed by individuals or other organizations, check the licensing before using them.

- Although application language configurations have been updated and messages added in various languages, the views are only rendered in English. There are no errors thrown at runtime and yet it doesn't work as expected.

  For Play to determine the language used from a request, it is required that the request should be an implicit one. Ensure that all the defined actions within the application make use of implicit requests.

  Another possibility can be that the Accept-Language header could be missing. This will be added by updating the browser settings.

- Will a compilation error occur when a message that doesn't have a mapping in the language resources is accessed?

  No, a compilation error occurs if an undefined message is being accessed. You can implement this mechanism if required or use something from the open source plugins if they're available and meet your requirements.

Summary

In this chapter, we saw how to create views using Twirl and the various helper methods provided by Play. We have built different kinds of views: reusable templates or widgets and forms. We also saw how to support multiple languages in our Play application using the built-in i18n API.

In the next chapter, we will cover how to handle data transactions available in Play, and also gain insights into how to effectively design your models.

5
Working with Data

The MVC approach talks about the model, view, and controller. We have seen views and controllers in detail in the previous chapters and neglected models to quite an extent. Models are an important part of MVC; the changes made to a model are reflected in the views and controllers using them.

Web applications are incomplete without data transactions. This chapter is about designing models and handling DB transactions in Play.

In this chapter, we will cover the following topics:

- Models
- JDBC
- Anorm
- Slick
- ReactiveMongo
- A Cache API

Introducing models

A **model** is a domain object, which maps to database entities. For example, a social networking application has users. The users can register, update their profile, add friends, post links, and so on. Here, the user is a domain object and each user will have corresponding entries in the database. Therefore, we could define a user model in the following way:

```
case class User(id: Long,
                loginId: String,
                name: Option[String],
                dob: Option[Long])
```

```
object User { def register (loginId: String,...) = {…}
...
}
```

Earlier, we defined a model without using a database:

```
case class Task(id: Int, name: String)

object Task {

  private var taskList: List[Task] = List()

  def all: List[Task] = {
    taskList
  }

  def add(taskName: String) = {
    val lastId: Int = if (!taskList.isEmpty) taskList.last.id else 0
    taskList = taskList ++ List(Task(lastId + 1, taskName))
  }

  def delete(taskId: Int) = {
    taskList = taskList.filterNot(task => task.id == taskId)
  }
}
```

The task list example had a `Task` model but it was not bound to a database, keeping things simpler. At the end of this chapter, we will be able to back it up with a database.

JDBC

Accessing the DB using **Java Database Connectivity (JDBC)** is common in applications using relational DBs. Play provides a plugin to manage the JDBC connection pool. The plugin internally uses BoneCP (`http://jolbox.com/`), a fast **Java Database Connection pool (JDBC pool)** library.

To use the plugin, a dependency in the build file should be added:

```
val appDependencies = Seq(jdbc)
```

The plugin supports H2, SQLite, PostgreSQL, MySQL, and SQL. Play is bundled with an H2 database driver, but to use any of the other databases we should add a dependency on its corresponding driver:

```
val appDependencies = Seq( jdbc,
"mysql" % "mysql-connector-java" % "5.1.18",...)
```

The plugin exposes the following methods:

- `getConnection`: It accepts the name of the database it should get the connection for and whether any statement executed using this connection should commit automatically or not. If a name is not provided, it fetches the connection for database with the default name.

- `withConnection`: It accepts a block of code that should be executed using a JDBC connection. Once the block is executed, the connection is released. Alternatively, it accepts the name of the database.

- `withTransaction`: It accepts a block of code that should be executed using a JDBC transaction. Once the block is executed, the connection and all its created statements are released.

How does the plugin know the details of the database? The details of the database can be set in `conf/application.conf`:

```
db.default.driver=com.mysql.jdbc.Driver
db.default.url="jdbc:mysql://localhost:3306/app"
db.default.user="changeme"
db.default.password="changeme"
```

The first part, `db`, is a set of properties, which are used by the DBPlugin. The second part is the name of the database, `default` in the example, and the last part is the name of the property.

For MySQL and PostgreSQL, we could include the user and password in the URL:

```
db.default.url="mysql://user:password@localhost:3306/app"
db.default.url="postgres://user:password@localhost:5432/app"
```

For additional JDBC configurations, refer to `https://www.playframework.com/documentation/2.3.x/SettingsJDBC`.

Now that we've enabled and configured the the JDBC plugin, we can connect to a SQL-like database and execute queries:

```
def fetchDBUser = Action {
    var result = "DB User:"
    val conn = DB.getConnection()
    try{
      val rs = conn.createStatement().executeQuery("SELECT USER()")
      while (rs.next()) {
        result += rs.getString(1)
      }
    } finally {
      conn.close()
```

```
      }
    Ok(result)
  }
```

Alternatively, we can use the `DB.withConnection` helper, which manages the DB connection:

```
def fetchDBUser = Action {
    var result = "DB User:"
    DB.withConnection { conn =>
      val rs = conn.createStatement().executeQuery("SELECT USER()")
      while (rs.next()) {
        result += rs.getString(1)
      }
    }
    Ok(result)
  }
```

Anorm

Anorm is a module in Play that supports interactions with the database using a plain SQL.

Anorm exposes methods to query the SQL database and parse the result as Scala objects, built in as well as custom.

The objective behind Anorm as stated on the Play website (https://www.playframework.com/documentation/2.3.x/ScalaAnorm) is:

Using JDBC is a pain, but we provide a better API

We agree that using the JDBC API directly is tedious, particularly in Java. You have to deal with checked exceptions everywhere and iterate over and over around the ResultSet to transform this raw dataset into your own data structure.

We provide a simpler API for JDBC; using Scala you don't need to bother with exceptions, and transforming data is really easy with a functional language. In fact, the goal of the Play Scala SQL access layer is to provide several APIs to effectively transform JDBC data into other Scala structures.

You don't need another DSL to access relational databases

SQL is already the best DSL for accessing relational databases. We don't need to invent something new. Moreover the SQL syntax and features can differ from one database vendor to another.

If you try to abstract this point with another proprietary SQL like DSL you will have to deal with several dialects dedicated for each vendor (like Hibernate ones), and limit yourself by not using a particular database's interesting features.

Play will sometimes provide you with pre-filled SQL statements, but the idea is not to hide the fact that we use SQL under the hood. Play just saves typing a bunch of characters for trivial queries, and you can always fall back to plain old SQL.

A typesafe DSL to generate SQL is a mistake

Some argue that a type safe DSL is better since all your queries are checked by the compiler. Unfortunately the compiler checks your queries based on a meta-model definition that you often write yourself by mapping your data structure to the database schema.

There are no guarantees that this meta-model is correct. Even if the compiler says that your code and your queries are correctly typed, it can still miserably fail at runtime because of a mismatch in your actual database definition.

Take control of your SQL code

Object Relational Mapping works well for trivial cases, but when you have to deal with complex schemas or existing databases, you will spend most of your time fighting with your ORM to make it generate the SQL queries you want.

Writing SQL queries yourself can be tedious for a simple 'Hello World' application, but for any real-life application, you will eventually save time and simplify your code by taking full control of your SQL code.

When developing an application using Anorm, its dependency should be specified explicitly, since it is a separate module in Play (starting from Play 2.1):

```
val appDependencies = Seq(
        jdbc,
        anorm
)
```

Let's picture our user model in MySQL. The table can be defined as follows:

```
CREATE TABLE `user` (
  `id` int(11) NOT NULL AUTO_INCREMENT,
  `login_id` varchar(45) NOT NULL,
  `password` varchar(50) NOT NULL,
  `name` varchar(45) DEFAULT NULL,
  `dob` bigint(20) DEFAULT NULL,
  `is_active` tinyint(1) NOT NULL DEFAULT '1',
  PRIMARY KEY (`id`),
  UNIQUE KEY `login_id_UNIQUE` (`login_id`),
  UNIQUE KEY `id_UNIQUE` (`id`)
) ENGINE=InnoDB
```

Now let's look at the different queries we will make in this table. The queries will be as follows:

- `Insert`: This query includes adding a new user
- `Update`: This query includes updating the profile, password, and so on
- `Select`: This query includes fetching one or more user's details, based on particular criteria

Assume that when a user requests to delete his account from our application, we do not delete the user from the database, but instead mark the user's status as inactive. Therefore, we will not use any delete queries.

Using Anorm, we could have the `userId` autogenerated as follows:

```
DB.withConnection {
  implicit connection =>
  val userId  = SQL"""INSERT INTO user(login_id,password,name,
  dob) VALUES($loginId,$password,$name,$dob)""".executeInsert()
  userId
}
```

Here, `loginId`, `password`, `name`, and `dob` are variables that are replaced in the query at runtime. Anorm builds only `java.sql.PreparedStatements`, which prevents SQL injection.

The SQL method returns an object of the `SimpleSql` type and is defined as follows:

```
implicit class SqlStringInterpolation(val sc: StringContext)
  extends AnyVal {
  def SQL(args: ParameterValue*) = prepare(args)

  private def prepare(params: Seq[ParameterValue]) = {
    // Generates the string query with "%s" for each parameter
placeholder
    val sql = sc.parts.mkString("%s")

    val (ns, ps): (List[String], Map[String, ParameterValue]) =
        namedParams(params)

      SimpleSql(SqlQuery(sql, ns), ps,
        defaultParser = RowParser(row => Success(row)))
    }
}
```

`SimpleSql` is used to represent a query in an intermediate format. Its constructor is as follows:

```
case class SimpleSql[T](sql: SqlQuery, params: Map[String,
  ParameterValue], defaultParser: RowParser[T]) extends Sql { … }
```

The `executeInsert` method fetches `PreparedStatement` from the `SimpleSql` object using its `getFilledStatement` method. Then the `getGeneratedKeys()` method of `PreparedStatement` is executed.

The `getGeneratedKeys` method results in an autogenerated key, created as a result of executing the statement in which it is called. If no key is created, it returns an empty object.

Now let's use Anorm to update a user's password:

```
DB.withConnection {
    implicit connection =>
SQL"""UPDATE user SET password=$password WHERE id =
  $userId""".executeUpdate()
}
```

The `executeUpdate` method works similar to `executeInsert`. The difference is that it calls the `executeUpdate` method of the `PreparedStatement`, instead of `getGeneratedKeys`.

The `executeUpdate` method returns a count of affected rows for the **Data Manipulation Language (DML)** statements. If the SQL statement is of the other types, such as **Data Definition Language (DDL)**, it returns 0.

Now let's try to fetch the details of all registered users. If we want the resulting rows to be parsed as user objects, we should define a parser. The parser for a user will be as follows:

```
def userRow:RowParser[User] = {
    get[Long]("id") ~
      get[String]("login_id") ~
      get[Option[String]]("name") map {
      case id ~ login_id ~ name  =>  User(id, login_id, name)
    }
  }
```

In most queries, we will not need the password and date of birth, so we can exclude them from the user `RowParser` default.

A query using this parser can be shown in this way:

```
DB.withConnection {
  implicit connection =>
  val query = "SELECT id,login_id,name FROM user"
  SQL(query).as(userRow.*)
}
```

The `.*` symbol indicates that the result should have one or more rows similar to its common interpretation in regular expressions. Similarly, the `.+` symbol can be used when we expect the result to consist of zero or more rows.

If you're using an older version of Scala where string interpolations are not supported, the queries would be written in this way:

```
DB.withConnection {
  implicit connection =>
val insertQuery  = """INSERT INTO
  user(login_id,password,name,
  |dob) VALUES({loginId},{password},{name},{dob})"""
    .stripMargin
val userId = SQL(insertQuery).on(
  'loginId -> loginId,
  'password -> password,
  'name -> name,
  'dob -> dob).executeInsert()
userId
}
```

The on method updates the query with the parameter map passed to it. It is defined for `SimpleSql` in the following way:

```
def on(args: NamedParameter*): SimpleSql[T] =
    copy(params = this.params ++ args.map(_.tupled))
```

Please refer to the Play documentation (`http://www.playframework.com/documentation/2.3.x/ScalaAnorm`) and the Anorm API documentation (`http://www.playframework.com/documentation/2.3.x/api/scala/index.html#anorm.package`) for more use casess and details.

Slick

According to Slick's website (`http://slick.typesafe.com/doc/2.1.0/introduction.html#what-is-slick`):

Slick is Typesafe's modern database query and access library for Scala. It allows you to work with stored data almost as if you were using Scala collections while at the same time giving you full control over when a database access happens and which data is transferred. You can also use SQL directly.

When using Scala instead of raw SQL for your queries you benefit from compile-time safety and compositionality. Slick can generate queries for different backend databases including your own, using its extensible query compiler.

We can use Slick in our Play application through the play-slick plugin. The plugin provides some additional features for the use of Slick in a Play application. According to `https://github.com/playframework/`, play-slick consists of three features:

- A wrapper DB object that uses the datasources defined in the Play config files, and pulls them from a connection pool. It is there so it is possible to use Slick sessions in the same fashion as you would Anorm JDBC connections. There are some smart caching and load balancing that make your connections to your DB perform better.

- A DDL plugin that reads Slick tables and automatically creates schema updates on reload. This is useful in particular for demos and to get started.

- A wrapper to use play Enumeratees together with Slick

To use it, we need to add the following library dependency in the build file:

```
"com.typesafe.play" %% "play-slick" % "0.8.1"
Let's see how we can define user operations using Slick.
```

First, we need to define the schema in Scala. This can be done by mapping the required tables to case classes. For our user table, the schema can be defined as:

```
case class SlickUser(id: Long, loginId: String, name: String)

class SlickUserTable(tag: Tag) extends Table[SlickUser](tag, "user") {
  def id = column[Long]("id", O.PrimaryKey, O.AutoInc)

  def loginId = column[String]("login_id")

  def name = column[String]("name")

  def dob = column[Long]("dob")

  def password = column[String]("password")

  def * = (id, loginId, name) <>(SlickUser.tupled,
    SlickUser.unapply)
}
```

`Table` is a Slick trait and its columns are specified through the `column` method. The following types are supported for a column:

- **Numeric types**: These include `Byte`, `Short`, `Int`, `Long`, `BigDecimal`, `Float`, and `Double`

- **Date types**: These include `java.sql.Date`, `java.sql.Time`, and `java.sql.Timestamp`

- **UUID type:** This includes `java.util.UUID`

- **LOB types**: These include `java.sql.Blob`, `java.sql.Clob`, and `Array[Byte]`

- **Other types**: These include `Boolean`, `String`, and `Unit`

The `column` method accepts column constraints, such as `PrimaryKey`, `Default`, `AutoInc`, `NotNull`, and `Nullable`.

The `*` method is mandatory for every table and is similar to `RowParser`.

Now we can define a `TableQuery` Slick using this and use it to query a database. There are simple methods available for performing equivalent DB operations. We can define the methods in the Anorm object using the play-slick wrapper along with the Slick API:

```
object SlickUserHelper {
  val users = TableQuery[SlickUserTable]

  def add(loginId: String,
          password: String,
          name: String = "anonymous",
          dateOfBirth: DateTime): Long = {

    play.api.db.slick.DB.withSession { implicit session =>
      users.map(p => (p.loginId, p.name, p.dob, p.password))
        .returning(users.map(_.id))
        .insert((loginId, name, dateOfBirth.getMillis, password))
    }
  }

  def updatePassword(userId: Long,
                     password: String) = {

    play.api.db.slick.DB.withSession { implicit session =>
      users.filter(_.id === userId)
```

```
        .map(u => u.password)
        .update(password)
    }
  }

  def getAll: Seq[SlickUser] = {
    play.api.db.slick.DB.withSession { implicit session =>
      users.run
    }
  }
}
```

The `run` method is equivalent to calling `SELECT *`.

For more details on this, refer to the Slick (`http://slick.typesafe.com/doc/2.1.0/`) and the play-slick documentation (`https://github.com/playframework/play-slick`).

ReactiveMongo

A lot of applications these days use a NoSQL database as a result of unstructured data, write scalability, and so on. MongoDB is one such database. According to its website (`http://docs.mongodb.org/manual/core/introduction/`):

> *MongoDB is an open source document database that provides high performance, high availability, and automatic scaling.*
>
> *Key features of MongoDB are:*
>
> *High performance*
>
> *High availability (automatic failover, data redundancy)*
>
> *Automatic scaling (horizontal scalability)*

ReactiveMongo is a Scala driver for MongoDB that supports non-blocking and asynchronous I/O operations. There is a plugin for the Play Framework called Play-ReactiveMongo. It is not a Play plugin but it's supported and maintained by the team of ReactiveMongo.

 This section requires prior knowledge of MongoDB, so please refer to `https://www.mongodb.org/`.

To use it, we need to do the following:

1. Include it as a dependency in the build file:

   ```
   libraryDependencies ++= Seq(
     "org.reactivemongo" %% "play2-reactivemongo" %
       "0.10.5.0.akka23"
   )
   ```

2. Include the plugin in `conf/play.plugins`:

   ```
   1100:play.modules.reactivemongo.ReactiveMongoPlugin
   ```

3. Add the MongoDB server details in `conf/application.conf`:

   ```
   mongodb.servers = ["localhost:27017"]
   mongodb.db = "your_db_name"
   mongodb.credentials.username = "user"
   mongodb.credentials.password = "pwd"
   ```

   Alternatively, use the following:

   ```
   mongodb.uri = "mongodb://user:password@localhost:
   27017/your_db_name"
   ```

Let's see usage of the plugin with a sample application. We may come across an instance in our application where we allow users to monitor activities on their devices in the form of heat sensors, smoke detectors, and so on.

Before using the device with our application installed on it, the device should be registered with this application. Each device has `ownerId`, `deviceId`, its configuration, and product information. So, let's assume that, on registration, we get a JSON in this format:

```
{
"deviceId" : "aghd",
"ownerId" : "someUser@someMail.com"
"config" : { "sensitivity" : 4, …},
"info" : {"brand" : "superBrand","os" : "xyz","version" : "2.4", …}
}
```

Once a device is registered, the owner can update the configuration or agree to update the product's software. Updating software is handled by the device company, and we only need to update the details in our application.

The queries to the database will be:

- `Insert`: This query includes registering a device
- `Update`: This query includes updating device configuration or information
- `Delete`: This query occurs when a device is unregistered
- `Select`: This query occurs when an owner wishes to view the details of the device

Using Reactive Mongo, the device registration will be:

```
def registerDevice(deviceId: String,
                   ownerId: String,
                   deviceDetails: JsObject): Future[LastError] = {

    var newDevice = Json.obj("deviceId" -> deviceId, "ownerId" ->
      ownerId.trim)
    val config = (deviceDetails \ "configuration").asOpt[JsObject]
    val metadata = (deviceDetails \ "metadata").asOpt[JsObject]
    if (!config.isDefined)
      newDevice = newDevice ++ Json.obj("configuration" ->
        Json.parse("{}"))
    if (!metadata.isDefined)
      newDevice = newDevice ++ Json.obj("metadata" ->
        Json.parse("{}"))

    collection.insert[JsValue](newDevice)
  }
```

In this snippet, we've built a JSON object from the available device details and inserted it in `devices`. Here, the collection is defined as follows:

```
def db = ReactiveMongoPlugin.db

def collection = db.collection("devices")
```

The insert command accepts the data and its type:

```
The db operations for fetching a device or removing it are simple,def
fetchDevice(deviceId: String): Future[Option[JsObject]]
= {
    val findDevice = Json.obj("deviceId" -> deviceId)
    collection.find(findDevice).one[JsObject]
  }

  def removeDeviceById(deviceId: String): Future[LastError] = {
```

```
    val removeDoc = Json.obj("deviceId" -> deviceId)
    collection.remove[JsValue](removeDoc)
  }
```

This leaves us with just the update query. An update is triggered for a single property of configuration or information, that is, the request has just one field and its new value is this:

```
{ "sensitivity": 4.5}
```

Now, a query to update this would be:

```
    def updateConfiguration(deviceId: String,
                     ownerId: String,
                 updatedField: JsObject) = {
    val property = updatedField.keys.head
    val propertyValue = updatedField.values.head
    val toUpdate = Json.obj(s"configuration.$property" ->
      propertyValue)
    val setData = Json.obj("$set" -> toUpdate)
    val documentToUpdate = Json.obj("deviceId" -> deviceId,
      "ownerId" -> ownerId)
    collection.update[JsValue, JsValue](documentToUpdate, setData)
  }
```

When we wish to update a field for a given document in MongoDB, we should add the updated data to the $set field in the query. For example, an equivalent MongoDB query would be as follows:

```
db.devices.update(
    { deviceId: "aghd" ,"ownerId" : "someUser@someMail.com"},
    { $set: { "configuration.sensitivity": 4.5 } }
)
```

The Cache API

Caching in a web application is the process of storing dynamically generated items, whether these are data objects, pages, or parts of a page, in memory at the initial time they are requested. This can later be reused if subsequent requests for the same data are made, thereby reducing response time and enhancing user experience. One can cache or store these items on the web server or other software in the request stream, such as the proxy server or browser.

Play has a minimal cache API, which uses EHCache. As stated on its website (http://ehcache.org/):

> **Ehcache** *is an open source, standards-based cache for boosting performance, offloading your database, and simplifying scalability. It's the most widely-used Java-based cache because it's robust, proven, and full-featured. Ehcache scales from in-process, with one or more nodes, all the way to mixed in-process/out-of-process configurations with terabyte-sized caches.*

It provides caching for presentation layers as well as application-specific objects. It is easy to use, maintain, and extend.

> To use the default cache API within a Play application, we should declare it as a dependency as follows:
>
> ```
> libraryDependencies ++= Seq(cache)
> ```

Using the default cache API is similar to using a mutable `Map[String, Any]`:

```
Cache.set("userSession", session)

val maybeSession: Option[UserSession] =
  Cache.getAs[UserSession]("userSession")

Cache.remove("userSession")
```

This API is made available through `EHCachePlugin`. The plugin is responsible for creating an instance of EHCache CacheManager with an available configuration on starting the application, and shutting it down when the application is stopped. We will discuss Play plugins in detail in *Chapter 13, Writing Play Plugins*. Basically, `EHCachePlugin` handles all the boilerplate required to use EHCache in an application and `EhCacheImpl` provides the methods to do so, such as `get`, `set`, and `remove`. It is defined as follows:

```
class EhCacheImpl(private val cache: Ehcache) extends CacheAPI {

  def set(key: String, value: Any, expiration: Int) {
    val element = new Element(key, value)
    if (expiration == 0) element.setEternal(true)
    element.setTimeToLive(expiration)
    cache.put(element)
  }

  def get(key: String): Option[Any] = {
    Option(cache.get(key)).map(_.getObjectValue)
```

```
    }

    def remove(key: String) {
      cache.remove(key)
    }
  }
```

> By default, the plugin looks for ehcache.xml in the conf directory
> and, if the file does not exist, the default configuration provided by
> the ehcache-default.xml framework is loaded.
>
> It is also possible to specify the location of the ehcache
> configuration when starting the application using the ehcache.
> configResource argument.

The Cache API also simplifies handling a cache for results from requests on both
the client and server side of the application. Adding EXPIRES and etag headers can
be used to manipulate the client-side cache, while on the server side the results are
cached so that its corresponding action is not computed for each call.

For example, we can cache the result of the request used to fetch details of
inactive users:

```
def getInactiveUsers = Cached("inactiveUsers") {

  Action {

    val users = User.getAllInactive

    Ok(Json.toJson(users))

  }

}
```

However, what if we want this to get updated every hour? We just need to specify
the duration explicitly:

```
def getInactiveUsers = Cached("inactiveUsers").default(3600) {
  Action {
    val users = User.getAllInactive
    Ok(Json.toJson(users))
  }
}
```

All of this is handled by the `Cached` case class and its companion object. The case class is defined as follows:

```
case class Cached(key: RequestHeader => String, caching:
  PartialFunction[ResponseHeader, Duration]) { ... }
```

The companion object provides commonly required methods to generate cached instances, such as cache action based on its status, and so on.

The `apply` method in cached calls the `build` method, which is defined as follows:

```
def build(action: EssentialAction)(implicit app: Application) =
  EssentialAction { request =>
    val resultKey = key(request)
    val etagKey = s"$resultKey-etag"

    // Has the client a version of the resource as fresh as the last
one we served?
    val notModified = for {
      requestEtag <- request.headers.get(IF_NONE_MATCH)
      etag <- Cache.getAs[String](etagKey)
      if requestEtag == "*" || etag == requestEtag
    } yield Done[Array[Byte], Result](NotModified)

    notModified.orElse {
      // Otherwise try to serve the resource from the cache, if it has
not yet expired
      Cache.getAs[Result](resultKey).map(Done[Array[Byte], Result](_))
    }.getOrElse {
      // The resource was not in the cache, we have to run the
underlying action
      val iterateeResult = action(request)

      // Add cache information to the response, so clients can cache
its content
      iterateeResult.map(handleResult(_, etagKey, resultKey, app))
    }
  }
```

It simply checks if the result was modified or not. If it hasn't been, it tries to get the result from the `Cache`. If the result does not exist in the cache, it fetches it from the action and adds it to the `Cache` using the `handleResult` method. The `handleResult` method is defined as follows:

```
private def handleResult(result: Result, etagKey: String,
  resultKey: String, app: Application): Result = {
  cachingWithEternity.andThen { duration =>
```

```
// Format expiration date according to http standard
val expirationDate = http.dateFormat.print
  (System.currentTimeMillis() + duration.toMillis)
  // Generate a fresh ETAG for it
  val etag = expirationDate // Use the expiration date as ETAG

  val resultWithHeaders = result.withHeaders(ETAG -> etag,
    EXPIRES -> expirationDate)

  // Cache the new ETAG of the resource
  Cache.set(etagKey, etag, duration)(app)
  // Cache the new Result of the resource
  Cache.set(resultKey, resultWithHeaders, duration)(app)

  resultWithHeaders
}.applyOrElse(result.header, (_: ResponseHeader) => result)
}
```

If a duration is specified, it returns that else it returns the default duration of one year.

The `handleResult` method simply takes the result, adds `etag`, expires headers, and then adds the result with the given key to `Cache`.

Troubleshooting

The following section covers some common scenarios:

- Anorm throws an error at the `SqlMappingError` runtime (too many rows when you're expecting a single one), even though the query resulted in expected behavior. It is an insert query using "on duplicate key update".

  This can happen when such a query is being executed using `executeInsert`. The `executeInsert` method should be used when we need to return an autogenerated key. If we are updating some fields through a duplicate key, it means that we do not actually need the key. We could use `executeUpdate` to add a check if one row has been updated. For example, we may want to update the wishlist table, which tracks what a user has wished for:

```
DB.withConnection {
      implicit connection => {

  val updatedRows = SQL"""INSERT INTO wish_list (user_id,
    product_id, liked_at) VALUES
    ($userId,$productId,$likedAt)
```

```
    ON DUPLICATE KEY UPDATE liked_at=$likedAt,
      is_deleted=false """.executeUpdate()

  updatedRows == 1
  }
}
```

- Can we use multiple databases for a single application?

  Yes, it is possible to use a different database of the same as well as a different kind. If an application requires this, we can use two or more different relational or NoSQL databases or a combination of both. For example, the application may store its user data in SQL (as we already know the format of the user data) and the information about THE user's devices in MongoDB (since the devices are from different vendors, the format of their data can change).

- Anorm does not throw a compilation error when a query has an incorrect syntax. Is there a configuration to enable this?

  It has been developed with the aim of using SQL queries in the code without any hassle. The developers are expected to pass correct queries to Anorm methods. To ensure that such errors do not occur at runtime, developers can execute the query locally and use it in the code if it succeeds. Alternatively, there are some third-party plugins that provide a typesafe DSL and can be used instead of Anorm if they meet the requirement, such as play-slick or scalikejdbc-play-support (`https://github.com/scalikejdbc/scalikejdbc-play-support`)

- Is it possible to use another caching mechanism?

  Yes, it is possible to extend support for any other cache, such as OSCache, SwarmCache, MemCached, and so on, or a custom one by writing a plugin similar to EHCachePlugin. Some of the popular caching mechanisms already have Play plugins developed by individuals and/or other organizations. For example, play2-memcached (`https://github.com/mumoshu/play2-memcached`) and Redis plugin (`https://github.com/typesafehub/play-plugins/tree/master/redis`).

Summary

In this chapter, we saw different ways of persisting application data in an application built using the Play Framework. In doing so, we have seen two contrasting approaches: one using a relational DB and the other using a NoSQL DB. To persist in a relational DB, we looked at how the Anorm module and the JDBC plugin work. To use a NoSQL database (MongoDB) for our application's backend, we used the Play plugin for ReactiveMongo. In addition to this, we saw how the Play Cache API can be used and how it works.

In the next chapter, we will be learning all about handling data streams in Play.

6
Reactive Data Streams

In particular circumstances, our application may be required to handle huge file uploads. This can be done by putting all of these in the memory, by creating a temporary file, or by acting directly on the stream. Out of these three, the last option works the best for us, as it removes I/O stream limitations (such as blocking, memory, and threads) and also eliminates the need to buffer (that is, acting on input at the rate needed).

Handling huge file uploads belongs to the set of unavoidable operations that can be heavy on resources. Some other tasks that belong to the same category are processing real-time data for monitoring, analysis, bulk data transfers, and processing large datasets. In this chapter, we will discuss the Iteratee approach used to handle such situations. This chapter covers the basics of handling data streams with a brief explanation of the following topics:

- Iteratees
- Enumerators
- Enumeratees

This chapter may seem intense at times but the topics discussed here will be helpful for some of the following chapters.

Basics of handling data streams

Consider that we connected a mobile device (such as a tablet, phone, MP3 player, and so on) to its charger and plugged it in. The consequences of this can be as follows:

- The device's battery starts charging and continues to do so until the occurrence of one of the other options

- The device's battery is completely charged and minimal power is drawn by the device to continue running

- The device's battery can not be charged due to malfunctioning of the device

Here, the power supply is the source, the device is the sink, while the charger is the channel that enables transfer of energy from the source to the sink. The processing or task performed by the device is that of charging its battery.

Well, this covers most of the Iteratee approach without any of the usual jargon. Simply put, the power supply represents a data source, the charger acts as the Enumerator, and the device as the Iteratee.

Oops, we missed the Enumeratee! Suppose that the energy from a regular power supply is not compatible with the device; then, in this case, the charger generally has an internal component that performs this transformation. For example, converting from A.C. (alternating current) to D.C. (direct current). In such cases, the charger can be considered a combination of the Enumerator and the Enumeratee. The component that collects energy from the power supply acts like the Enumerator, and the other component that transforms the energy is similar to an Enumeratee.

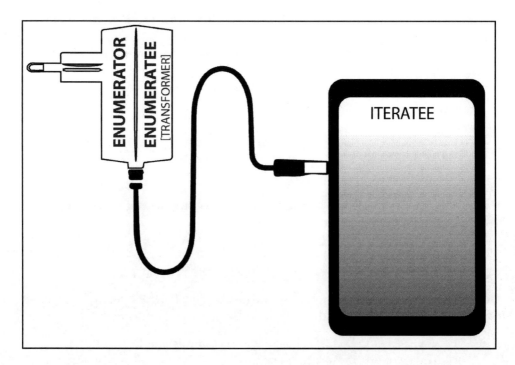

The concept of Iteratee, Enumerator, and Enumeratee originated from the Haskell library Iteratee I/O, which was developed by Oleg Kiselyov to overcome the problems faced with lazy I/O.

In Oleg's words, as seen on `http://okmij.org/ftp/Streams.html`:

> *Enumerator is an encapsulation of a data source, a stream producer – what folds an iteratee over the stream. An enumerator takes an iteratee and applies it to the stream data as they are being produced, until the source is depleted or the iteratee said it had enough. After disposing of buffers and other source-draining resources, enumerator returns the final value of the iteratee. Enumerator thus is an iteratee transformer.*

Iteratees are stream consumers and an Iteratee can be in one of the following states:

- *Completed or done*: The Iteratee has completed processing
- *Continuing*: The current element has been processed but the Iteratee is not done yet and can accept the next element
- *Error*: The Iteratee has encountered an error

> *Enumeratee is both a consumer and a producer, incrementally decoding the outer stream and producing the nested stream of decoded data.*

Although the enumerator knows how to get to the next element, it is completely unaware of the processing the Iteratee will perform on this element and vice versa.

Different libraries implement the Iteratee, Enumerator, and Enumeratee differently, based on these definitions. In the following sections, we will see how these are implemented in Play Framework and how we can use them in our application. Let's start with the Iteratee, as the Enumerator requires a one.

Iteratees

Iteratee is defined as a trait, `Iteratee[E, +A]`, where E is the input type and A is the result type. The state of an Iteratee is represented by an instance of `Step`, which is defined as follows:

```
sealed trait Step[E, +A] {

  def it: Iteratee[E, A] = this match {
    case Step.Done(a, e) => Done(a, e)
    case Step.Cont(k) => Cont(k)
    case Step.Error(msg, e) => Error(msg, e)
```

```
  }

}

object Step {

  //done state of an iteratee
  case class Done[+A, E](a: A, remaining: Input[E]) extends Step[E, A]

  //continuing state of an iteratee.
  case class Cont[E, +A](k: Input[E] => Iteratee[E, A]) extends
Step[E, A]

  //error state of an iteratee
  case class Error[E](msg: String, input: Input[E]) extends Step[E,
Nothing]
}
```

The input used here represents an element of the data stream, which can be empty, an element, or an end of file indicator. Therefore, Input is defined as follows:

```
sealed trait Input[+E] {
  def map[U](f: (E => U)): Input[U] = this match {
    case Input.El(e) => Input.El(f(e))
    case Input.Empty => Input.Empty
    case Input.EOF => Input.EOF
  }
}

object Input {

  //An input element
  case class El[+E](e: E) extends Input[E]

  // An empty input
  case object Empty extends Input[Nothing]

  // An end of file input
  case object EOF extends Input[Nothing]

}
```

An Iteratee is an immutable data type and each result of processing an input is a new Iteratee with a new state.

To handle the possible states of an Iteratee, there is a predefined helper object for each state. They are:

- Cont
- Done
- Error

Let's see the definition of the `readLine` method, which utilizes these objects:

```
def readLine(line: List[Array[Byte]] = Nil): Iteratee[Array[Byte],
String] = Cont {
    case Input.El(data) => {
      val s = data.takeWhile(_ != '\n')
      if (s.length == data.length) {
        readLine(s :: line)
      } else {
        Done(new String(Array.concat((s :: line).reverse: _*),
          "UTF-8").trim(), elOrEmpty(data.drop(s.length + 1)))
      }
    }
    case Input.EOF => {
      Error("EOF found while reading line", Input.Empty)
    }
    case Input.Empty => readLine(line)
  }
```

The `readLine` method is responsible for reading a line and returning an Iteratee. As long as there are more bytes to be read, the `readLine` method is called recursively. On completing the process, an Iteratee with a completed state (Done) is returned, else an Iteratee with state continuous (Cont) is returned. In case the method encounters EOF, an Iteratee with state Error is returned.

In addition to these, Play Framework exposes a companion Iteratee object, which has helper methods to deal with Iteratees. The API exposed through the Iteratee object is documented at https://www.playframework.com/documentation/2.3.x/api/scala/index.html#play.api.libs.iteratee.Iteratee$.

The Iteratee object is also used internally within the framework to provide some key features. For example, consider the request body parsers. The `apply` method of the `BodyParser` object is defined as follows:

```
def apply[T](debugName: String)(f: RequestHeader =>
Iteratee[Array[Byte], Either[Result, T]]): BodyParser[T] = new
  BodyParser[T] {
```

```
        def apply(rh: RequestHeader) = f(rh)
        override def toString = "BodyParser(" + debugName + ")"
}
```

So, to define `BodyParser[T]`, we need to define a method that accepts `RequestHeader` and returns an `Iteratee` whose input is an `Array[Byte]` and results in Either`[Result,T]`.

Let's look at some of the existing implementations to understand how this works.

The `RawBuffer` parser is defined as follows:

```
    def raw(memoryThreshold: Int): BodyParser[RawBuffer] =
        BodyParser("raw, memoryThreshold=" + memoryThreshold) { request =>
            import play.core.Execution.Implicits.internalContext
            val buffer = RawBuffer(memoryThreshold)
            Iteratee.foreach[Array[Byte]](bytes => buffer.push(bytes)).map {
                _ =>
                buffer.close()
                Right(buffer)
            }
    }
```

The `RawBuffer` parser uses `Iteratee.forEach` method and pushes the input received into a buffer.

The file parser is defined as follows:

```
    def file(to: File): BodyParser[File] = BodyParser("file, to=" +
        to) { request =>
            import play.core.Execution.Implicits.internalContext
            Iteratee.fold[Array[Byte], FileOutputStream](new
                FileOutputStream(to)) {
                (os, data) =>
                os.write(data)
                os
            }.map { os =>
                os.close()
                Right(to)
            }
    }
```

The file parser uses the `Iteratee.fold` method to create `FileOutputStream` of the incoming data.

Now, let's see the implementation of Enumerator and how these two pieces fit together.

Enumerator

Similar to the Iteratee, an **Enumerator** is also defined through a trait and backed by an object of the same name:

```
trait Enumerator[E] {
  parent =>
  def apply[A](i: Iteratee[E, A]): Future[Iteratee[E, A]]
  ...
}
object Enumerator{
def apply[E](in: E*): Enumerator[E] = in.length match {
    case 0 => Enumerator.empty
    case 1 => new Enumerator[E] {
      def apply[A](i: Iteratee[E, A]): Future[Iteratee[E, A]] =
        i.pureFoldNoEC {
        case Step.Cont(k) => k(Input.El(in.head))
        case _ => i
      }
    }
    case _ => new Enumerator[E] {
      def apply[A](i: Iteratee[E, A]): Future[Iteratee[E, A]] =
        enumerateSeq(in, i)
    }
  }
  ...
}
```

Observe that the `apply` method of the trait and its companion object are different. The `apply` method of the trait accepts `Iteratee[E, A]` and returns `Future[Iteratee[E, A]]`, while that of the companion object accepts a sequence of type `E` and returns an `Enumerator[E]`.

Now, let's define a simple data flow using the companion object's `apply` method; first, get the character count in a given `(Seq[String])` line:

```
val line: String = "What we need is not the will to believe, but
    the wish to find out."
val words: Seq[String] = line.split(" ")

val src: Enumerator[String] = Enumerator(words: _*)

val sink: Iteratee[String, Int] = Iteratee.fold[String,
   Int](0)((x, y) => x + y.length)
val flow: Future[Iteratee[String, Int]] = src(sink)

val result: Future[Int] = flow.flatMap(_.run)
```

The variable result has the `Future[Int]` type. We can now process this to get the actual count.

In the preceding code snippet, we got the result by following these steps:

1. Building an Enumerator using the companion object's `apply` method:

    ```
    val src: Enumerator[String] = Enumerator(words: _*)
    ```

2. Getting `Future[Iteratee[String, Int]]` by binding the Enumerator to an Iteratee:

    ```
    val flow: Future[Iteratee[String, Int]] = src(sink)
    ```

3. Flattening `Future[Iteratee[String,Int]]` and processing it:

    ```
    val result: Future[Int] = flow.flatMap(_.run)
    ```

4. Fetching the result from `Future[Int]`:

Thankfully, Play provides a shortcut method by merging steps 2 and 3 so that we don't have to repeat the same process every time. The method is represented by the `|>>>` symbol. Using the shortcut method, our code is reduced to this:

```
val src: Enumerator[String] = Enumerator(words: _*)
val sink: Iteratee[String, Int] = Iteratee.fold[String, Int](0)((x, y)
=> x + y.length)
val result: Future[Int] = src |>>> sink
```

Why use this when we can simply use the methods of the data type? In this case, do we use the `length` method of `String` to get the same value (by ignoring whitespaces)?

In this example, we are getting the data as a single `String` but this will not be the only scenario. We need ways to process continuous data, such as a file upload, or feed data from various networking sites, and so on.

For example, suppose our application receives heartbeats at a fixed interval from all the devices (such as cameras, thermometers, and so on) connected to it. We can simulate a data stream using the `Enumerator.generateM` method:

```
val dataStream: Enumerator[String] = Enumerator.generateM {
  Promise.timeout(Some("alive"), 100 millis)
}
```

In the preceding snippet, the `"alive"` String is produced every 100 milliseconds. The function passed to the `generateM` method is called whenever the Iteratee bound to the Enumerator is in the `Cont` state. This method is used internally to build enumerators and can come in handy when we want to analyze the processing for an expected data stream.

An Enumerator can be created from a file, `InputStream`, or `OutputStream`. Enumerators can be concatenated or interleaved. The Enumerator API is documented at `https://www.playframework.com/documentation/2.3.x/api/scala/index.html#play.api.libs.iteratee.Enumerator$`.

Using the Concurrent object

The `Concurrent` object is a helper that provides utilities for using Iteratees, enumerators, and Enumeratees concurrently. Two of its important methods are:

* **Unicast**: It is useful when sending data to a single iterate.
* **Broadcast**: It facilitates sending the same data to multiple Iteratees concurrently.

Unicast

For example, the character count example in the previous section can be implemented as follows:

```
val unicastSrc = Concurrent.unicast[String](
  channel =>
    channel.push(line)
)


val unicastResult: Future[Int] = unicastSrc |>>> sink
```

The `unicast` method accepts the `onStart`, `onError`, and `onComplete` handlers. In the preceding code snippet, we have provided the `onStart` method, which is mandatory. The signature of unicast is this:

```
def unicast[E](onStart: (Channel[E]) ⊠ Unit,
    onComplete: ⊠ Unit = (),
    onError: (String, Input[E]) ⊠ Unit = (_: String, _: Input[E])
      => ())(implicit ec: ExecutionContext): Enumerator[E] {…}
```

So, to add a log for errors, we can define the `onError` handler as follows:

```
val unicastSrc2 = Concurrent.unicast[String](
    channel => channel.push(line),
    onError = { (msg, str) => Logger.error(s"encountered $msg for
    $str")}
    )
```

Now, let's see how broadcast works.

Broadcast

The broadcast [E] method creates an enumerator and a channel and returns a (Enumerator [E] , Channel [E]) tuple. The enumerator and channel thus obtained can be used to broadcast data to multiple Iteratees:

```scala
val (broadcastSrc: Enumerator[String], channel:
  Concurrent.Channel[String]) = Concurrent.broadcast[String]
private val vowels: Seq[Char] = Seq('a', 'e', 'i', 'o', 'u')

def getVowels(str: String): String = {
  val result = str.filter(c => vowels.contains(c))
  result
}

def getConsonants(str: String): String = {
  val result = str.filterNot(c => vowels.contains(c))
  result
}

val vowelCount: Iteratee[String, Int] = Iteratee.fold[String,
  Int](0)((x, y) => x + getVowels(y).length)

val consonantCount: Iteratee[String, Int] =
  Iteratee.fold[String, Int](0)((x, y) => x +
  getConsonants(y).length)

val vowelInfo: Future[Int]  = broadcastSrc |>>> vowelCount
val consonantInfo: Future[Int]  = broadcastSrc |>>>
  consonantCount

words.foreach(w => channel.push(w))
channel.end()

vowelInfo onSuccess { case count => println(s"vowels:$count")}
consonantInfo onSuccess { case count =>
  println(s"consonants:$count")}
```

Enumeratees

Enumeratee is also defined using a trait and its companion object with the same Enumeratee name.

It is defined as follows:

```
trait Enumeratee[From, To] {
...
def applyOn[A](inner: Iteratee[To, A]): Iteratee[From,
  Iteratee[To, A]]

def apply[A](inner: Iteratee[To, A]): Iteratee[From, Iteratee[To,
  A]] = applyOn[A](inner)
...
}
```

An Enumeratee transforms the Iteratee given to it as input and returns a new Iteratee. Let's look at a method that defines an Enumeratee by implementing the applyOn method. An Enumeratee's flatten method accepts Future[Enumeratee] and returns an another Enumeratee, which is defined as follows:

```
def flatten[From, To](futureOfEnumeratee:
  Future[Enumeratee[From, To]]) = new Enumeratee[From, To] {
  def applyOn[A](it: Iteratee[To, A]): Iteratee[From,
    Iteratee[To, A]] =
    Iteratee.flatten(futureOfEnumeratee.map
      (_.applyOn[A](it))(dec))
}
```

In the preceding snippet, applyOn is called on the Enumeratee whose future is passed and dec is defaultExecutionContext.

Defining an Enumeratee using the companion object is a lot simpler. The companion object has a lot of methods to deal with Enumeratees, such as map, transform, collect, take, filter, and so on. The API is documented at https://www.playframework. com/documentation/2.3.x/api/scala/index.html#play.api.libs.iteratee. Enumeratee$.

Let's define an Enumeratee by working through a problem. The example we used in the previous section to find the count of vowels and consonants will not work correctly if a vowel is capitalized in a sentence, that is, the result of `src |>>>` `vowelCount` will be incorrect when the `line` variable is defined as follows:

```
val line: String = "What we need is not the will to believe, but the
wish to find out.".toUpperCase
```

To fix this, let's alter the case of all the characters in the data stream to lowercase. We can use an Enumeratee to update the input provided to the Iteratee.

Now, let's define an Enumeratee to return a given string in lowercase:

```
val toSmallCase: Enumeratee[String, String] =
  Enumeratee.map[String] {
  s => s.toLowerCase
}
```

There are two ways to add an Enumeratee to the dataflow. It can be bound to the following:

- Enumerators
- Iteratees

Binding an Enumeratee to an Enumerator

An Enumeratee can be bound to an enumerator by using the enumerator's `through` method, which returns a new Enumerator and is composed using the given enumeratee.

Updating the example to include an Enumeratee, we get this:

```
val line: String = "What we need is not the will to believe, but the
wish to find out.".toUpperCase
val words: Seq[String] = line.split(" ")

val src: Enumerator[String] = Enumerator(words: _*)

private val vowels: Seq[Char] = Seq('a', 'e', 'i', 'o', 'u')
def getVowels(str: String): String = {
  val result = str.filter(c => vowels.contains(c))
  result
}

src.through(toSmallCase) |>>> vowelCount
```

The `through` method is an alias for the `&>` method and is defined for an enumerator, so the last statement can also be rewritten as follows:

```
src &> toSmallCase |>>> vowelCount
```

Binding an Enumeratee to an Iteratee

Now, let's implement the same flow by binding the enumeratee to the Iteratee. This can be done using the enumeratee's `transform` method. The `transform` method transforms the given Iteratee and results in a new Iteratee. Modifying the flow according to this, we get the following:

```
src |>>> toSmallCase.transform(vowelCount)
```

The enumeratee's `transform` method has a `&>>` symbolic alias. Using this, we can rewrite the flow as follows:

```
src |>>> toSmallCase &>> vowelCount
```

In addition to the fact that enumeratees can be bound to either Enumerators or Iteratees, different Enumeratees can be also be combined if the output type of one is the same as the input type of the other. For example, assume we have a `filterVowel` Enumeratee that filters out the vowels, as demonstrated in the following code:

```
val filterVowel: Enumeratee[String, String] =
  Enumeratee.map[String] {
  str => str.filter(c => vowels.contains(c))
}
```

Combining `toSmallCase` and `filterVowel` is possible since the output type of `toSmallCase` is a `String` and the input type of `filterVowel` is also a `String`. To do this, we use the Enumeratee's `compose` method:

```
toSmallCase.compose(filterVowel)
```

Now, let's rewrite the flow by using this:

```
src |>>> toSmallCase.compose(filterVowel) &>> sink
```

Here, `sink` is defined as follows:

```
val sink: Iteratee[String, Int] = Iteratee.fold[String,
  Int](0)((x, y) => x + y.length)
```

Like the `transform` and `compose` methods, this also has a `><>` symbolic alias. Let's define the flow using all the symbols instead of method names in the following way:

```
src |>>> toSmallCase ><> filterVowel &>> sink
```

We can add another enumeratee that computes the length of `String` and uses `Iteratee`, which simply sums up the lengths:

```
val toInt: Enumeratee[String, Int] = Enumeratee.map[String] {
  str => str.length
}
val sum: Iteratee[Int, Int] = Iteratee.fold[Int, Int](0)((x, y)
  => x + y)
```

src |>>> toSmallCase ><> filterVowel ><> toInt &>> sum

FLOW		REPRESENTATION
i/p⊸(ENUMERATOR)⊸o/p ⟶ (ITERATEE/ ENUMERATEE) i/p		ENUMERATOR |>>> ENUMERATEE/ITERATEE
i/p⊸(ENUMERATEE)⊸o/p ⟶ (ENUMERATEE) i/p		ENUMERATEE ><> ENUMERATEE
i/p⊸(ENUMERATEE)⊸o/p ⟶ (ITERATEE) i/p		ENUMERATEE &<> ITERATEE

In the preceding snippet, we had to use a different iterator that accepts data of the `Int` type, since our `toInt` enumeratee transforms the `String` input to `Int`.

This concludes the chapter. Define a few data flows to get familiar with the API. Start with simpler data flows, such as extracting all the numbers or words in a given paragraph, and then complicate them gradually.

Summary

In this chapter, we discussed the concept of Iteratees, Enumerators, and Enumeratees. We also saw how they were implemented in Play Framework and used internally. This chapter also walked you through a simple example to illustrate how data flow can be defined using the API exposed by Play Framework.

In the next chapter, we will explore the features provided in a Play application through a global plugin.

7
Playing with Globals

Sometimes web applications require application-wide objects that live beyond the request-response life cycle, such as database connections, application configuration, shared objects, and cross-cutting concerns (authentication, error handling, and so on). Consider the following:

- Ensuring that the database used by the application is defined and accessible.
- Notify through e-mail or any other service when the application is receiving unexpected heavy traffic.
- Logging the different requests served by the application. These logs can later be used to analyze user behavior.
- Restricting certain facilities on the web application by time. For example, some food ordering apps take orders only between 11 a.m. to 8 p.m., while all requests to build orders at any other time will be blocked and a message about the timings will be displayed.
- Generally, when a user sends an e-mail and the recipient's email ID is incorrect or not in use, the sender is notified about the failure in delivering the e-mail only after 12 to 24 hrs. In this duration, further attempts are made to send the e-mail.

Applications with in-app sales allow users to retry with the same or different payment options when payment has been declined for various reasons.

In a Play Framework app, by convention, all of these various concerns can be managed through GlobalSettings.

In this chapter, we will discuss the following topics:

- GlobalSettings
- Application life cycle
- Request-response life cycle

GlobalSettings

Every Play application has a global object which can be used to define application-wide objects. It can also be used to customize the application's life cycle and the request-response life cycle.

The global object for an application can be defined by extending the trait `GlobalSettings`. By default, the name of the object is expected to be `Global` and it is assumed to be in the `app` directory. This can be changed by updating `application.global` in the `conf/application.conf` property. For example, if we wish to use a file with `AppSettings` in the `app/com/org` name:

```
application.global=app.com.org.AppSettings
```

The `GlobalSettings` trait has methods that can be used to interrupt both the application's life cycle and the request-response life cycle. We will see its methods as and when required in the following sections.

Now, let's see how this works.

An app developed through the Play Framework is represented by an instance of the `Application` trait, since its creation and the build is to be handled by the framework itself.

The `Application` trait is extended by `DefaultApplication` and `FakeApplication`. `FakeApplication` is a helper that tests Play applications and we will see more of it in *Chapter 9, Testing*. `DefaultApplication` is defined as follows:

```
class DefaultApplication(
    override val path: File,
    override val classloader: ClassLoader,
    override val sources: Option[SourceMapper],
    override val mode: Mode.Mode) extends Application with
WithDefaultConfiguration with WithDefaultGlobal with
WithDefaultPlugins
```

The `WithDefaultConfiguration` and `WithDefaultPlugins` traits are used to initialize the application's configuration and plugin objects, respectively. The `WithDefaultGlobal` trait is the one responsible for setting the correct global object for the application. It is defined as follows:

```
trait WithDefaultGlobal {
  self: Application with WithDefaultConfiguration =>

  private lazy val globalClass =
    initialConfiguration.getString
    ("application.global").getOrElse
    (initialConfiguration.getString("global").map { g =>
```

```
   Play.logger.warn("`global` key is deprecated, please change
   `global` key to `application.global`")
   g
}.getOrElse("Global"))

lazy private val javaGlobal: Option[play.GlobalSettings] = try {
  Option(self.classloader.loadClass
  (globalClass).newInstance().asInstanceOf[play.GlobalSettings])
} catch {
  case e: InstantiationException => None
  case e: ClassNotFoundException => None
}

lazy private val scalaGlobal: GlobalSettings = try {
  self.classloader.loadClass(globalClass +
  "$").getDeclaredField("MODULE$").get(null).
  asInstanceOf[GlobalSettings]
} catch {
  case e: ClassNotFoundException if !initialConfiguration.getString
  ("application.global").isDefined => DefaultGlobal
  case e if initialConfiguration.getString
  ("application.global").isDefined => {
    throw initialConfiguration.reportError("application.global",
      s"Cannot initialize the custom Global object
      ($globalClass) (perhaps it's a wrong reference?)",
      Some(e))
  }
}

private lazy val globalInstance: GlobalSettings =
  Threads.withContextClassLoader(self.classloader) {
  try {
    javaGlobal.map(new j.JavaGlobalSettingsAdapter
      (_)).getOrElse(scalaGlobal)
  } catch {
    case e: PlayException => throw e
    case e: ThreadDeath => throw e
    case e: VirtualMachineError => throw e
    case e: Throwable => throw new PlayException(
      "Cannot init the Global object",
      e.getMessage,
      e
    )
```

```
      }
    }

    def global: GlobalSettings = {
      globalInstance
    }
  }
```

The `globalInstance` object is the `global` object to be used for this application. It is set to `javaGlobal` or `scalaGlobal`, whichever is applicable to the application. If the application does not have custom Global object configured for the application, the application's `global` is set to `DefaultGlobal`. It is defined as:

```
object DefaultGlobal extends GlobalSettings
```

The life cycle of an application

An application's life cycle has two states: **running** and **stopped**. These are times when the state of the application changes. At times, we need to perform some operations right before or after a state change has occurred or is about to occur.

Play applications use a Netty server. For this, a class with the same name is used. It is defined as follows:

```
class NettyServer(appProvider: ApplicationProvider,
  port: Option[Int],
  sslPort: Option[Int] = None,
  address: String = "0.0.0.0",
  val mode: Mode.Mode = Mode.Prod) extends Server with
    ServerWithStop { … }
```

This class is responsible for binding or bootstrapping the application to the server.

The `ApplicationProvider` trait is defined as follows:

```
trait ApplicationProvider {
  def path: File
  def get: Try[Application]
  def handleWebCommand(requestHeader: play.api.mvc.RequestHeader):
    Option[Result] = None
}
```

An implementation of `ApplicationProvider` must create and initialize an application. Currently, there are three different implementations of `ApplicationProvider`. They are as follows:

- `StaticApplication`: This is to be used in the production mode (the mode where code changes do not affect an already running application).

- `ReloadableApplication`: This is to be used in the development mode (this is a mode where continuous compilation is enabled so that developers can see the impact of changes in an application as and when they are saved, if the application is up and running).

- `TestApplication`: This is to be used in the testing mode (the mode where a fake application is started through the tests).

`StaticApplication` and `ReloadableApplication` both initialize a `DefaultApplication`. `StaticApplication` is used in the production mode and is defined as follows:

```
class StaticApplication(applicationPath: File) extends
ApplicationProvider {

  val application = new DefaultApplication(applicationPath, this.
getClass.getClassLoader, None, Mode.Prod)

  Play.start(application)

  def get = Success(application)
  def path = applicationPath
}
```

`ReloadableApplication` is used in the development mode but, since the class definition is huge, let's see the relevant lines of code where `DefaultApplication` is used:

```
class ReloadableApplication(buildLink: BuildLink, buildDocHandler:
  BuildDocHandler) extends ApplicationProvider {
...
// First, stop the old application if it exists
    Play.stop()

    val newApplication = new DefaultApplication(reloadable.path,
      projectClassloader, Some(new SourceMapper {
        def sourceOf(className: String, line: Option[Int]) = {
          Option(buildLink.findSource(className,
            line.map(_.asInstanceOf[java.lang.Integer])
            .orNull)).flatMap {
```

```
        case Array(file: java.io.File, null) => Some((file,
          None))
        case Array(file: java.io.File, line:
          java.lang.Integer) => Some((file, Some(line)))
        case _ => None
        }
      }
        }), Mode.Dev) with DevSettings {
          import scala.collection.JavaConverters._
          lazy val devSettings: Map[String, String] =
            buildLink.settings.asScala.toMap
        }

      Play.start(newApplication)
  ...
  }
```

For `StaticApplication`, the application is created and started just once whereas, in the case of `ReloadableApplication`, the existing application is stopped and a new one is created and started. The `ReloadableApplication` is for the development mode, so as to allow developers to make changes and see them reflected without the hassle of reloading the application manually every time.

The usage of `ApplicationProvider` and `NettyServer` is similar to this:

```
val appProvider = new ReloadableApplication(buildLink,
  buildDocHandler)
val server = new NettyServer(appProvider, httpPort, httpsPort,
  mode = Mode.Dev)
```

In the following section, we will discuss the methods available in GlobalSettings, which enable us to hook into the application's life cycle.

Meddling with an application's life cycle

Consider that our application has the following specifications:

- Prior to starting the application, we need to ensure that the /opt/dev/ appName directory exists and is accessible by the application. A method in our application called `ResourceHandler.initialize` does this task.

- Create the required schema on startup using the `DBHandler.createSchema` method. This method does not drop the schema if it already exists. This ensures that the application's data is not lost on restarting the application and the schema is generated only when the application is first started.

- Create e-mail application logs when the application is stopped using the `Mailer.sendLogs` method. This method sends the application logs as an attachment in an e-mail to the `emailId` set in a configuration file as `adminEmail`. This is used to track the cause for the application's shutdown.

Play provides methods that allow us to hook into the application's life cycle and complete such tasks. The `GlobalSettings` trait has methods that assist in doing so. These can be overridden by the `Global` object, if required.

To cater to the specifications of the application described earlier, all we need to do in a Play application is define a `Global` object, as shown here:

```
object Global extends GlobalSettings {

  override def beforeStart(app: Application): Unit = {
    ResourceHandler.initialize
  }

  override def onStart(app: Application):Unit={
    DBHandler.createSchema
  }

  override def onStop(app: Application): Unit = {
    Mailer.sendLogs
  }
}
```

The `ResourceHandler.initialize`, `DBHandler.createSchema`, and `Mailer.sendLogs` methods are specific to our application and are defined by us, not provided by Play.

Now that we know how to hook into the application's life cycle, let's scrutinize how it works.

Digging deeper into the application's life cycle we can see that all the implementations of `ApplicationProvider` use the `Play.start` method to initialize an application. The `Play.start` method is defined as follows:

```
def start(app: Application) {

    // First stop previous app if exists
    stop()

    _currentApp = app

    // Ensure routes are eagerly loaded, so that the reverse routers
are correctly
```

```
// initialized before plugins are started.
app.routes
Threads.withContextClassLoader(classloader(app)) {
  app.plugins.foreach(_.onStart())
}

app.mode match {
  case Mode.Test =>
  case mode => logger.info("Application started (" + mode + ")")
}

}
```

This method ensures that each plugin's `onStart` method is called right after the application is set as `_currentApp`. `GlobalPlugin`, is added by default to all the Play applications, and is defined as:

```
class GlobalPlugin(app: Application) extends Plugin {

  // Call before start now
  app.global.beforeStart(app)

  // Called when the application starts.
  override def onStart() {
    app.global.onStart(app)
  }

  //Called when the application stops.
  override def onStop() {
    app.global.onStop(app)
  }

}
```

In the preceding snippet, `app.global` refers to the GlobalSettings defined for the application. Therefore, the GlobalPlugin ensures that the appropriate methods of the application's GlobalSettings are called.

The `beforeStart` method is called on initialization of the plugin.

Now, we just need to figure out how `onStop` is called. Once an application is stopped, `ApplicationProvider` does not have control, so the Java runtime shutdown hook is used to ensure that certain tasks are executed once the application is stopped. Here is a look at the relevant lines from the `NettyServer.createServer` method:

```
Runtime.getRuntime.addShutdownHook(new Thread {
      override def run {
        server.stop()
      }
    })
```

Here, runtime is java.lang.Runtime (Java docs for the same are available at `http://docs.oracle.com/javase/7/docs/api/java/lang/Runtime.html`) and the server is an instance of NettyServer. NettyServer's `stop` method is defined as:

```
override def stop() {

    try {
      Play.stop()
    } catch {
      case NonFatal(e) => Play.logger.error("Error while stopping
        the application", e)
    }

    try {
      super.stop()
    } catch {
      case NonFatal(e) => Play.logger.error("Error while stopping
        logger", e)
    }

    mode match {
      case Mode.Test =>
      case _ => Play.logger.info("Stopping server...")
    }

    // First, close all opened sockets
    allChannels.close().awaitUninterruptibly()

    // Release the HTTP server
    HTTP.foreach(_._1.releaseExternalResources())

    // Release the HTTPS server if needed
```

```
HTTPS.foreach(_._1.releaseExternalResources())

mode match {
  case Mode.Dev =>
    Invoker.lazySystem.close()
    Execution.lazyContext.close()
  case _ => ()
  }
}
```

Here, the `Invoker.lazySystem.close()` call is used to shut down the ActorSystem used internally within a Play application. The `Execution.lazyContext.close()` call is to shut down Play's internal `ExecutionContext`.

The `Play.stop` method is defined as follows:

```
def stop() {
  Option(_currentApp).map { app =>
    Threads.withContextClassLoader(classloader(app)) {
      app.plugins.reverse.foreach { p =>
        try {
          p.onStop()
        } catch { case NonFatal(e) => logger.warn("Error stopping
          plugin", e) }
      }
    }
  }
  _currentApp = null
}
```

This method calls the `onStop` method of all the registered plugins in reverse order, so the GlobalPlugin's `onStop` method is called and it eventually calls the `onStop` method of the `GlobalSetting` defined for the application. Any errors encountered in this process are logged as warnings since the application is going to be stopped.

We can now add any task within the application's life cycle, such as creating database schemas before starting, initializing global objects, or scheduling jobs (using Akka Scheduler or Quartz, and so on) on starting and cleaning temporary data when stopping.

We've covered the application's life cycle, now let's look into the request-response life cycle.

The request-response life cycle

The Play Framework uses Netty by default, so requests are received by NettyServer.

Netty allows a variety of actions including custom coding through handlers. We can define a handler that transforms a request into a desired response and provides it to Netty when bootstrapping the application. To integrate a Play app with Netty, `PlayDefaultUpstreamHandler` is used.

 For additional information on requests used in Netty, refer to Netty docs at `http://netty.io/wiki/user-guide-for-4.x.html` and Netty ChannelPipeline docs at `http://netty.io/4.0/api/io/netty/channel/ChannelPipeline.html`.

`PlayDefaultUpstreamHandler` extends `org.jboss.netty.channel.SimpleChannelUpstreamHandler` to handle both HTTP and WebSocket requests. It is used when bootstrapping the application to Netty in the following way:

```
val defaultUpStreamHandler = new PlayDefaultUpstreamHandler(this,
   allChannels)
```

The `messageReceived` method of `SimpleChannelUpStreamHandler` is responsible for acting on the received request. `PlayDefaultUpstreamHandler` overwrites this so that requests are sent to our application. This method is too long (around 260 lines, including comments and blank lines), so we will only look at relevant blocks here.

First, a Play `RequestHeader` is created for the message received and its corresponding action is found:

```
val (requestHeader, handler: Either[Future[Result], (Handler,
   Application)]) = Exception.allCatch[RequestHeader].either {
     val rh = tryToCreateRequest
            // Force parsing of uri
            rh.path
            rh
          }.fold(
           e => {
             //Exception Handling
             ...
           },
           rh => server.getHandlerFor(rh) match {
             case directResult @ Left(_) => (rh, directResult)
```

```
                case Right((taggedRequestHeader, handler,
                    application)) => (taggedRequestHeader,
                    Right((handler, application)))
        }
    )
```

In the preceding snippet, the `tryToCreateRequest` method results in `RequestHeader` and any exceptions encountered in this process are handled. The action for the `RequestHeader` `rh` is then fetched through `server.getHandlerFor(rh)`. Here, a `server` is an instance of the server trait and the `getHandlerFor` method utilizes the application's `global` object and its `onRequestReceived` method:

```
try {
        applicationProvider.get.map { application =>
            application.global.onRequestReceived(request) match {
                case (requestHeader, handler) => (requestHeader, handler,
                    application)
            }
        }
    } catch {
  //Exception Handling
...
}
```

In the `messageReceived` method of `PlayDefaultUpstreamHandler`, the action obtained from `server.getHandlerFor` is eventually called, resulting in a response.

Most of the interactions of `PlayDefaultUpStreamHandler` with the application are through its global object. In the following section, we will see the methods available in GlobalSettings related to the request-response life cycle.

Fiddling with the request-response life cycle

The `GlobalSettings` trait has methods related to different stages of the application's life cycle as well as its request-response life cycle. Using the request-related hooks, we can define business logic when a request is received, when an action is not found for the request, and so on.

The request-related methods are as follows:

- `onRouteRequest`: This uses a router to identify the action for a given `RequestHeader`

- `onRequestReceived`: This results in `RequestHeader` and its action. Internally, it calls the `onRouteRequest` method

- `doFilter`: This adds a filter to the application
- `onError`: This is a method that handles exceptions when processing
- `onHandlerNotFound`: This is used when a RequestHeader's corresponding action cannot be found
- `onBadRequest`: This is used internally when the request body is incorrect
- `onRequestCompletion`: This is used to perform operations after a request has been processed successfully

Manipulating requests and their responses

In some applications, it is mandatory to filter, modify, redirect requests, and their responses. Consider these examples:

- Requests for any service must have headers that contain session details and user identities except for instances, such as logins, registers, and forgetting passwords
- All requests made for a path starting with `admin` must be restricted by the user role
- Redirect requests to regional sites if possible (such as Google)
- Add additional fields to the request or response

The `onRequestReceived`, `onRouteRequest`, `doFilter`, and `onRequestCompletion` methods can be used to intercept the request or its response and manipulate them as per requirements.

Let's look at the `onRequestReceived` method:

```
def onRequestReceived(request: RequestHeader): (RequestHeader,
  Handler) = {
    val notFoundHandler =
      Action.async(BodyParsers.parse.empty)
      (this.onHandlerNotFound)
    val (routedRequest, handler) = onRouteRequest(request) map {
      case handler: RequestTaggingHandler =>
        (handler.tagRequest(request), handler)
      case otherHandler => (request, otherHandler)
    } getOrElse {
    // We automatically permit HEAD requests against any GETs without
the need to
    // add an explicit mapping in Routes
      val missingHandler: Handler = request.method match {
        case HttpVerbs.HEAD =>
```

```
            new HeadAction(onRouteRequest(request.copy(method =
                HttpVerbs.GET)).getOrElse(notFoundHandler))
            case _ =>
                notFoundHandler
        }
        (request, missingHandler)
    }


    (routedRequest, doFilter(rh => handler)(routedRequest))
}
```

It fetches the corresponding handler for a given `RequestHeader` using the `onRouteRequest` and `doFilter` methods. If no handler is found, the result from `onHandlerNotFound` is sent.

Since the `onRequestReceived` method plays a critical role in how the requests are processed, sometimes it may be simpler to override the `onRouteRequest` method.

The `onRouteRequest` method is defined as follows:

```
def onRouteRequest(request: RequestHeader): Option[Handler] =
    Play.maybeApplication.flatMap(_.routes.flatMap {
        router =>
            router.handlerFor(request)
    })
```

Here, the router is the application's `router` object. By default, it is the generated object created from `conf/routes` on compilation. A router extends the `Router.Routes` trait and the `handlerFor` method is defined in this trait.

Let's try to implement a solution for blocking requests to services other than `login`, `forgotPassword`, and `register` if the request header does not have the session and user details. We can do so by overriding `onRouteRequest`:

```
override def onRouteRequest(requestHeader: RequestHeader) = {
    val path = requestHeader.path

    val pathConditions = path.equals("/") ||
        path.startsWith("/register") ||
        path.startsWith("/login") ||
        path.startsWith("/forgot")

    if (!pathConditions) {
        val tokenId = requestHeader.headers.get("Auth-Token")
        val userId = requestHeader.headers.get("Auth-User")
        if (tokenId.isDefined && userId.isDefined) {
```

```
        val isValidSession = SessionDetails.validateSession
          (SessionDetails(userId.get.toLong, tokenId.get))
        if (isValidSession) {
          super.onRouteRequest(request)
        }
        else Some(controllers.SessionController.invalidSession)
      }
      else {
        Some(controllers.SessionController.invalidSession)
      }
    }
    else {
      super.onRouteRequest(request)
    }
  }
```

First, we check if the requested path has restricted access. If so, we check if the necessary headers are available and valid. Only then is the corresponding `Handler` returned, else `Handler` for an invalid session is returned. A similar approach can be followed if we need to control the access based on the user's role.

We can also use the `onRouteRequest` method to provide compatibility for older deprecated services. For example, if the older version of the application had a GET `/user/:userId` service that has now been modified to `/api/user/:userId`, and there are other applications that rely on this application, our application should support requests for both the paths. However, the routes file only lists the new paths and services, which means that we should handle these before attempting to access the application's supported routes:

```
override def onRouteRequest(requestHeader: RequestHeader) = {
  val path = requestHeader.path

  val actualPath = getSupportedPath(path)
  val customRequestHeader = requestHeader.copy(path = actualPath)

  super.onRouteRequest(customRequestHeader)
}
```

The `getSupportedPath` is a custom method that gives a new path for a given old path. We create a new `RequestHeader` with the updated fields and forward this to the following methods instead of the original `RequestHeader`.

Similarly, we could add/modify the headers or any other field(s) of `RequestHeader`.

The `doFilter` method can be used to add filters, similar to those shown in *Chapter 2, Defining Actions*:

```
object Global extends GlobalSettings {
  override def doFilter(action: EssentialAction): EssentialAction
    = HeadersFilter.noCache(action)
}
```

Alternatively, we can extend the `WithFilters` class instead of `GlobalSettings`:

```
object Global extends WithFilters(new CSRFFilter()) with
GlobalSettings
```

The `WithFilters` class extends `GlobalSettings` and overrides the `doFilter` method with the `Filter` passed in its constructor. It is defined as follows:

```
class WithFilters(filters: EssentialFilter*) extends GlobalSettings {
  override def doFilter(a: EssentialAction): EssentialAction = {
    Filters(super.doFilter(a), filters: _*)
  }
}
```

The `onRequestCompletion` method can be used to perform specific tasks after a request has been processed. For example, suppose that the application needs a requirement to persist data from specific GET requests, such as Search. This can come in handy to understand and analyze what the users are looking for in our application. Persisting information from requests prior to fetching data can considerably increase the response time and hamper user experience. Therefore, it will be better if this is done after the response has been sent:

```
override def onRequestCompletion(requestHeader: RequestHeader) {
  if(requestHeader.path.startsWith("/search")){
    //code to persist request parameters, time, etc
  }}
```

Tackling errors and exceptions

An application cannot exist without handling errors and exceptions. Based on the business logic, the way they are handled may differ from application to application. Play provides certain standard implementations which can be overridden in the application's global object. The `onError` method is called when an exception occurs and is defined as follows:

```
def onError(request: RequestHeader, ex: Throwable):
  Future[Result] = {
  def devError = views.html.defaultpages.devError
  (Option(System.getProperty("play.editor"))) _
```

```
  def prodError = views.html.defaultpages.error.f
  try {
    Future.successful(InternalServerError
    (Play.maybeApplication.map {
      case app if app.mode == Mode.Prod => prodError
      case app => devError
    }.getOrElse(devError) {
      ex match {
        case e: UsefulException => e
        case NonFatal(e) => UnexpectedException(unexpected =
          Some(e))
      }
    }))
  } catch {
    case NonFatal(e) => {
      Logger.error("Error while rendering default error page",
        e)
      Future.successful(InternalServerError)
    }
  }
}
```

`UsefulException` is an abstract class, which extends `RuntimeException`. It is extended by the `PlayException` helper. The default implementation of `onError` (in the previous code snippet) simply checks whether the application is in the production mode or in the development mode and sends the corresponding view as `Result`. This method results in the `defaultpages.error` or `defaultpages.devError` view.

Suppose we want to send a response with a status 500 and the exception instead. We can easily do so by overriding the `onError` method:

```
override def onError(request: RequestHeader, ex: Throwable) = {
  log.error(ex)
  InternalServerError(ex.getMessage)
}
```

The `onHandlerNotFound` method is called when a user sends a request with a path that is not defined in `conf/routes`. It is defined as follows:

```
def onHandlerNotFound(request: RequestHeader): Future[Result] = {
  Future.successful(NotFound(Play.maybeApplication.map {
    case app if app.mode != Mode.Prod =>
      views.html.defaultpages.devNotFound.f
    case app => views.html.defaultpages.notFound.f
```

```
  }.getOrElse(views.html.defaultpages.devNotFound.f)(request,
    Play.maybeApplication.flatMap(_.routes))))
}
```

It sends a view as a response, depending on the mode in which the application was started. In the development mode, the view contains an error message, which tells us that an action is defined for the route and the list of supported paths with the request type. We can override this, if required.

The `onBadRequest` method is called in the following situations:

- The request is sent and its corresponding action has a different content type
- Some of the parameters are missing in the request sent and, when parsing, the request throws an exception

It is defined as follows:

```
def onBadRequest(request: RequestHeader,
  error: String): Future[Result] = {
    Future.successful(BadRequest
      (views.html.defaultpages.badRequest(request, error)))
}
```

This method also sends a view in response but, in most applications, we would like to send `BadRequest` with the error message and not the view. This can be achieved by overriding the default implementation, as follows:

```
import play.api.mvc.{Result, RequestHeader,Results}
 override def onBadRequest(request: RequestHeader,
                           error: String): Future[Result] = {
    Future{
      Results.BadRequest(error)
    }
}
```

Summary

In this chapter, we saw the features provided to a Play application through a global plugin. By extending `GlobalSettings`, we can hook into the application's life cycle and perform various tasks at different phases. Apart from hooks used for the application life cycle, we have also discussed hooks for the request-response life cycle, through which we can intercept requests and responses and modify them, if required.

8
WebSockets and Actors

In this chapter, we will cover the following topics:

- Introduction to WebSockets
- Actor Model and Akka Actors
- WebSockets in Play: using Iteratees and Actors
- FrameFormatters

An introduction to WebSockets

Picture this:

A moviegoer is trying to purchase movie tickets online. He or she has selected the seats, entered the payment details, and submitted. He or she gets an error message saying that the tickets they tried to book have sold out.

Consider an application, which gives detailed information about the stock market and allows purchasing/selling stocks. When someone enters payment details and submits these details, they get an error saying that the purchase has been rejected as the price of the stock has now changed.

Initially, in applications where real-time data was required over HTTP, developers realized that they needed bidirectional communication between the client side and server side. It was generally implemented using one of the following approaches:

- **Polling**: Requests are sent from the client side at fixed and regular intervals. The server responds within a short span (less than 1 second or so) with a result for each request made.

- **Long-polling**: When a request is sent, the server does not respond with a result unless there has been a change in the state within a specified time period. A request is fired after a response is received from the server. Therefore, the client side makes repeated requests as and when it gets the response for the previous one.

- **Streaming**: A request to the server results in an open response, which is continuously updated and kept open indefinitely.

Although these approaches worked, using them led to some problems:

- It led to an increase in the number of TCP connections per client

- There was a high overhead of HTTP Header Overhead while mapping a response to its corresponding request on the client side

In 2011, a protocol that uses a single TCP connection for bidirectional traffic, WebSocket (RFC6455), was standardized by the **Internet Engineering Task Force (IETF)**. By September 20, 2012, the **World Wide Web Consortium (W3C)** came up with the specifications for a WebSocket API.

Unlike HTTP, there is no request-response cycle in a WebSocket. Once connected, the client and server can send messages to each other. The communication can be by server and by client, that is, a two-way full duplex communication.

According to the WebSocket API:

- A WebSocket connection can be established by invoking the constructor, such as `WebSocket(url, protocols)`

- Data can be sent to the server via a connection using the `send(data)` method

- Calling `close()` will result in closing the connection

- The following event handlers can be defined on the client side:

    ○ `onopen`

    ○ `onmessage`

    ○ `onerror`

    ○ `onclose`

A snippet using JavaScript is shown here:

```
var webSocket = new WebSocket('ws://localhost:9000');
webSocket.onopen = function () {
  webSocket.send("hello");
};
webSocket.onmessage = function (event) {
```

```
      console.log(event.data);
   };
   webSocket.onclose = function () {
      alert("oops!! Disconnected")
   }
```

WebSockets in Play

WebSockets cannot be defined using Action since they should be bidirectional. Play provides a helper to assist with WebSockets, which is documented at `https://www.playframework.com/documentation/2.3.x/api/scala/index.html#play.api.mvc.WebSocket$`.

 WebSockets, which are defined using the helper, use the Play server's underlying TCP port.

WebSockets can be defined similarly to Actions in Play applications. Starting from Play 2.3, a WebSocket helper finds a method to define WebSocket interactions using an Actor. However, before we learn more about the methods provided by the helper, let's take a small detour and get a little familiar with the **Actor Model** and **Akka Actors**.

Actor Model

Concurrency in programming can be achieved by using *Threads* which may include the risk of a lost update or a deadlock. The Actor Model facilitates concurrency by utilizing asynchronous communication.

According to the Actor Model, an actor is the fundamental unit of computation. It cannot exist independently, that is, it is always part of a specific actor system. An actor can send messages to one or more actors within its actor system if it knows the address of the other actor. It can also send messages to itself. The order in which the messages are sent or received cannot be guaranteed since the communication is asynchronous.

When an actor receives a message, it can do the following:

- Forward it to another actor whose address is known to it
- Create more actors
- Designate the action it will take for the next message

The Actor Model was first described in August 1973 in a publication by Carl Hewitt, Peter Bishop and Richard Steiger in the paper *A Universal Modular ACTOR Formalism for Artificial Intelligence*, which was a part of the International Joint Conference on Artificial Intelligence (IJCAI'73).

Introducing Akka Actors

Akka is a part of the Typesafe Reactive Platform, which is similar to the Play Framework. According to their website:

> *Akka is a toolkit and runtime used to build highly concurrent, distributed, and fault-tolerant event-driven applications on the JVM.*

Akka implements a version of the Actor Model, which is commonly called Akka Actors and is available for both Java and Scala. According to the Akka documentation, Actors give you:

- Simple and high-level abstractions for concurrency and parallelism
- Asynchronous, nonblocking, and highly performant event-driven programming model
- Very lightweight event-driven processes (several million actors per GB of heap memory)

Akka Actors are available as a library and can be used within a project by adding them into the dependencies:

```
libraryDependencies ++= Seq(
  "com.typesafe.akka" %% "akka-actor" % "2.3.4"
)
```

 Adding a dependency in Akka explicitly is not required in a Play project as Play uses Akka internally.

We can then define an actor by extending the Actor trait and defining the behavior in the `receive` method. Let's build an Actor, which reverses any string message it receives:

```
class Reverser extends Actor {

  def receive = {
    case s:String => println( s.reverse)
    case _ => println("Sorry, didn't quite understand that. I can only
process a String.")
  }
}

object Reverser {
  def props = Props(classOf[Reverser])
}
```

To use the actor, we first need to initialize `ActorSystem`:

```
val system = ActorSystem("demoSystem")
```

Now we can get a reference of the actor by using the `actorOf` method:

```
val demoActor = system.actorOf(Reverser.props, name = "demoActor")
```

This reference can then be used to send messages:

```
demoActor ! "Hello, How do u do?"
demoActor ! "Been Long since we spoke"
demoActor ! 12345
```

Now let's run the application and see what the actor does:

```
> run

[info] Compiling 1 Scala source to /AkkaActorDemo/target/scala-2.10/
classes...

[info] Running com.demo.Main

?od u od woH ,olleH

ekops ew ecnis gnoL neeB

Sorry, didn't quite understand that I can only process a String.
```

Suppose we wanted to define an Actor that accepted `minLength` and `MaxLength` as arguments, we would need to modify the `Reverser` class and its companion as follows:

```
class ReverserWithLimit(min:Int,max:Int) extends Actor {

  def receive = {
    case s:String if (s.length> min & s.length<max)=> println(
      s.reverse)
    case _ => println(s"Sorry, didn't quite understand that. I can
      only process a String of length $min-$max.")   }
}

object ReverserWithLimit {
  def props(min:Int,max:Int) = Props(classOf[Reverser],min,max)
}
```

For more details on Akka actors, refer to `http://akka.io/docs/`.

WebSocket using Iteratee

Let's define a WebSocket connection, which accepts strings and sends back the reverse of a string using **Iteratee**:

```
def websocketBroadcast = WebSocket.using[String] {
  request =>
    val (out, channel) = Concurrent.broadcast[String]
    val in = Iteratee.foreach[String] {
      word => channel.push(word.reverse)
    }
    (in, out)
}
```

The `WebSocket.using` method creates a WebSocket of a specific type using an Iteratee (inbound channel) and its corresponding enumerator (outbound channel). In the preceding code snippet, we return a tuple of the Iteratee in and the Enumerator out.

The `Concurrent` object is also a helper, which provides utilities to use Iteratees, Enumerators, and Enumeratees concurrently. The `broadcast[E]` method creates an Enumerator and a channel and returns a `(Enumerator[E], Channel[E])` tuple. The Enumerator and channel, thus obtained, can be used to broadcast data to multiple Iteratees.

After this, we need to bind it to a path in the routes file, which is similar to what we do for an Action:

```
GET          /ws                     controllers.Application.
websocketBroadcast
```

Now, using a browser plugin, such as simple WebSocket client for Chrome (refer to https://chrome.google.com/webstore/detail/simple-websocket-client/pfdhoblngboilpfeibdedpjgfnlcodoo), we can send messages through the WebSocket when an application is running, as shown here:

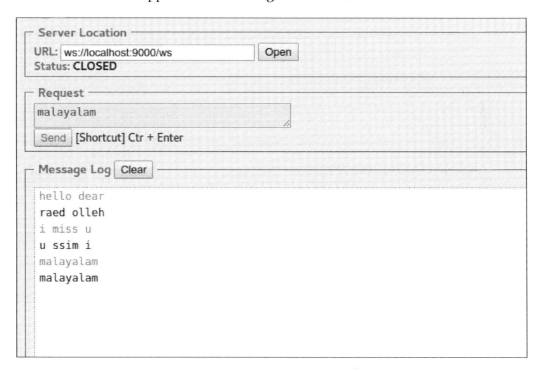

Since we do not use multiple Iteratees in our application, we can use `Concurrent.unicast`. This will require us to modify our code slightly:

```scala
def websocketUnicast = WebSocket.using[String] {
  request =>
    var channel: Concurrent.Channel[String] = null
    val out = Concurrent.unicast[String] {
      ch =>
        channel = ch
    }
    val in = Iteratee.foreach[String] {
      word => channel.push(word.reverse)
```

```
      }
      (in, out)
  }
```

Notice that, unlike the `broadcast` method, the `unicast` method does not return a tuple of enumerators and channels, but instead only provides an enumerator. We have to declare a channel variable and initialize it with null, so that it is accessible within the Iteratee. When the `unicast` method is called, it is set to the channel generated within the `unicast` method.

> The `unicast` method also allows us to define the `onComplete` and `onError` methods, but they are not aware of the Iteratee, that is, we cannot refer to the Iteratee within these methods.

This example is overtly simple and does not highlight the complications involved in defining and using Iteratees. Let's try a more challenging use case. Now, we might need to build a web application that lets users connect to their database and load/view data over a WebSocket. Given this condition, the frontend sends JSON messages.

Now the WebSocket can get any of the following messages:

- **Connection request**: It is a message that shows the information required to connect to a database (such as a host, port, user ID, and password)
- **Query string**: It is the query to be executed in the database
- **Disconnect request**: It is a message that closes a connection with the database

After this, the message is translated and sent to the **DBActor**, which sends back a status message or a result with row data, and is then translated to JSON and sent back by the WebSocket.

The response received from the DBActor can be one of the following:

- A successful connection
- Connection failure
- Query result
- Invalid query
- Disconnected

We can define a WebSocket handler for this scenario in the following manner:

```
def dbWebsocket = WebSocket.using[JsValue] {
    request =>
```

```
        WebSocketChannel.init
    }
```

Here, `WebSocketChannel` is an actor, which communicates with the DBActor and its companion object and is defined as follows:

```
object WebSocketChannel {
  def props(channel: Concurrent.Channel[JsValue]): Props =
    Props(classOf[WebSocketChannel], channel)

  def init: (Iteratee[JsValue, _], Enumerator[JsValue]) = {

    var actor: ActorRef = null
    val out = Concurrent.unicast[JsValue] {
      channel =>
        actor = Akka.system.actorOf
          (WebSocketChannel.props(channel))
    }

    val in = Iteratee.foreach[JsValue] {
      jsReq => actor ! jsReq
    }
    (in, out)
  }
}
```

`WebSocketChannel` is defined as follows:

```
class WebSocketChannel(wsChannel: Concurrent.Channel[JsValue])
  extends Actor with ActorLogging {

  val backend = Akka.system.actorOf(Props(classOf[DBActor]))

  def receive: Actor.Receive = {
    case jsRequest: JsValue =>
      backend ! convertJson(jsRequest)
    case x: DBResponse =>
      wsChannel.push(x.toJson)
  }
}
```

In the preceding code, `convertJson` translates `JsValue` to the format that is understood by the DBActor.

In the following section, we will implement the same application using the new WebSocket methods available in Play since the 2.3.x version.

WebSocket using Actors without Iteratees

The Play WebSocket API allows the use of Actors to define the behavior. Let's build the WebSocket application that replies with the reverse of a given String once it's connected. We can do this by slightly modifying our Reverser Actor to have an argument as the reference of the Actor to which it can/must send messages, as shown here:

```scala
class Reverser(outChannel: ActorRef) extends Actor {

    def receive = {
      case s: String => outChannel ! s.reverse
    }
}

object Reverser {
  def props(outChannel: ActorRef) = Props(classOf[Reverser],
    outChannel)
}
```

The `websocket` can then be defined in a controller as follows:

```scala
def websocket = WebSocket.acceptWithActor[String, String] {
  request => out =>
    Reverser.props(out)
}
```

Finally, we make an entry in the routes file:

```
GET          /wsActor                    controllers.Application.websocket
```

We can now send messages through the WebSocket when the application is running using a browser plugin.

Now, lets try to implement `dbWebSocket` using this method:

```scala
def dbCommunicator = WebSocket.acceptWithActor[JsValue, JsValue] {
    request => out =>
      WebSocketChannel.props(out)
}
```

Here, WebSocketChannel is defined as follows:

```
class WebSocketChannel(out: ActorRef)
  extends Actor with ActorLogging {

  val backend = Akka.system.actorOf(DBActor.props)
  def receive: Actor.Receive = {
    case jsRequest: JsValue =>
      backend ! convertJsonToMsg(jsRequest)
    case x:DBResponse =>
      out ! x.toJson
  }
}

object WebSocketChannel {
  def props(out: ActorRef): Props =
    Props(classOf[WebSocketChannel], out)
}
```

The convertJsonToMsg method is responsible for translating JSON to a format that is accepted by the DBActor.

Closing a WebSocket

When the WebSocket is closed, Play automatically stops the actor bound to it. This binding works in two ways: the WebSocket connection is closed when the underlying actor is killed. If there is a need to free any resources once the connection is closed, we can do so by overriding the actor's postStop method. In our example, we have initialized a DBActor within WebSocketChannel. We will need to ensure that it's killed once the WebSocket is closed, since each connection to the WebSocket will lead to the initialization of a DBActor. We can do so by sending it a poison pill, as shown here:

```
override def postStop() = {
  backend ! PoisonPill
}
```

Using FrameFormatter

Suppose that an incoming JSON has the same fields for every request, instead of parsing it every time; we can define an equivalent class in this way:

```
case class WebsocketRequest(reqType:String, message:String)
```

Now, we can define our WebSocket to translate the JSON message to a `WebSocketRequest` automatically. This is possible by specifying the data type for the `acceptWithActor` method:

```
def websocketFormatted = WebSocket.acceptWithActor
  [WebsocketRequest, JsValue]{
  request => out =>
  SomeActor.props(out)
}
```

However, for this to work as expected, we need two implicit values. The first is for translating incoming frames to `WebsocketRequest`, which requires a `JsValue` to the `WebSocketRequest` formatter:

```
implicit val requestFormat = Json.format[WebsocketRequest]
implicit val requestFrameFormatter =
  FrameFormatter.jsonFrame[WebsocketRequest]
```

Similarly, we can specify the types of the outgoing messages as well:

`FrameFormatter` is a helper and can convert `org.jboss.netty.handler.codec.http.websocketx.WebSocketFrame` to `play.core.server.websocket.Frames`.

> The WebSocket methods do not validate the format of data received automatically in the same manner as Action parsers. We will need to do this additionally, if required.

Troubleshooting

- What is the equivalent of interrupting `Actions` in `GlobalSettings` for `WebSockets`? What if we want to refuse a WebSocket connection when certain headers are missing? Something similar to the following code snippet didn't work as expected:

```
override def onRouteRequest(request: RequestHeader):
  Option[Handler] = {
    if(request.path.startsWith("/ws")){
      Option(controllers.Default.error)
    } else
      super.onRouteRequest(request)
  }
```

Interrupting WebSocket from the global object does not work as it does for Actions. However, there are other means of doing so: by using the `tryAccept` and `tryAcceptWithActor` methods. A WebSocket definition can be replaced by the following code:

```
def wsWithHeader = WebSocket.tryAccept[String] {
    rh =>
      Future.successful(rh.headers.get("token") match {
        case Some(x) =>
          var channel: Concurrent.Channel[String] = null
          val out = Concurrent.unicast[String] {
            ch =>
              channel = ch
          }
          val in = Iteratee.foreach[String] {
            word => channel.push(word.reverse)
          }
          Right(in, out)
        case _ => Left(Forbidden)
      })
  }
```

When using an Actor, define a WebSocket with the `tryAcceptWithActor` method:

```
def wsheaders = WebSocket.tryAcceptWithActor[String,
  String] {
    request =>
      Future.successful(request.headers.get("token") match {
        case Some(x) => Right(out => Reverser.props(out))
        case _ => Left(Forbidden)
      })
  }
```

In the preceding examples, we are only checking to see if there is a token header, but this can be updated to any other criteria.

- Does Play support wss?

  As of 2.3.x, there is no built-in support for wss. However, it's possible to use proxies, such as Nginx or HAProxy as the secure WebSocket (wss) endpoint and forward to an internal Play app with an insecure WebSocket endpoint.

Summary

We have learned a couple of things in this chapter. This chapter briefly covered the Actor Model and usage of Akka Actors in an application. In addition to this, we defined a WebSocket connection in a Play application with various constraints and requirements using two different approaches: the first one where we use Iteratees and Enumerators, and the second where we use Akka Actors.

In the next chapter, we will see the different ways in which we can test a Play application using **Specs2** and **ScalaTest**.

9
Testing

Testing is the process of cross-checking the implementation of an application/process. It brings its shortcomings out into the open. It can be extremely handy when you are upgrading/downgrading one or more dependencies. Tests can be classified into various categories based on different programming practices, but in this chapter, we will only discuss two types of tests:

- **Unit tests**: These are tests that check the functionality of a specific section of code
- **Functional tests**: These are tests that check a specific action, mostly written to verify working code with regard to a use case or scenario

In the following sections, we will see the different ways in which we can test a Play application using **Specs2** and **ScalaTest**.

> The tests using either of the Specs2 and ScalaTest libraries are similar. The major difference is in the keywords, syntax, and style. Since different developers can have different preferences, in this chapter, tests are defined using both libraries and for convenience. Most of the tests written using Specs2 have names ending with 'Spec', while those using ScalaTest end with 'Test'.

The setup for writing tests

Play is packaged with Specs2, since this is the library used internally for testing it. It provides support to test applications using Specs2 by default, that is, no additional library dependency is required.

Using `ScalaTest` earlier was difficult but now, Play also provides helpers for using ScalaTest. Although it is picked up from transitive dependencies, we need to add a library dependency to use the helper methods:

```
val appDependencies = Seq(
   "org.scalatestplus" %% "play" % "1.1.0" % "test"
)
```

 The 1.1.0 version of `org.scalatestplus.play` is compatible with Play 2.3.x. It is better to check the compatibility when working with another version of Play at `http://www.scalatest.org/plus/play/versions`.

Unit testing

Unit tests can be written as in any Scala project. For example, suppose we have a utility method `isNumberInRange` that takes a string and checks if it's a number in the range [0,3600]. It is defined as follows:

```
def isNumberInRange(x:String):Boolean = {
    val mayBeNumber = Try{x.toDouble}
    mayBeNumber match{
      case Success(n) => if(n>=0 && n<=3600) true else false
      case Failure(e) => false
    }
  }
```

Let's write a unit test to check this function using `Specs2`:

```
class UtilSpec extends Specification {

    "range method" should {

    "fail for Character String" in {
      Util.isNumberInRange("xyz") should beFalse
    }

    "fail for Java null" in {
      Util.isNumberInRange(null) should beFalse
    }

    "fail for Negative numbers" in {
      Util.isNumberInRange("-2") should beFalse
```

```
    }

    "pass for valid number" in {
      Util.isNumberInRange("1247") should beTrue
    }

    "pass for 0" in {
      Util.isNumberInRange("0") should beTrue
    }

    "pass for 3600" in {
      Util.isNumberInRange("3600") should beTrue
    }


  }
}
```

These scenarios can also be written using ScalaTest with slight modifications:

```
class UtilTest extends FlatSpec with Matchers {

  "Character String" should "not be in range" in {
    Util.isNumberInRange("xyz") should be(false)
  }

  "Java null" should "not be in range" in {
    Util.isNumberInRange(null) should be(false)
  }

  "Negative numbers" should "not be in range" in {
    Util.isNumberInRange("-2") should be(false)
  }

  "valid number" should "be in range" in {
    Util.isNumberInRange("1247") should be(true)
  }

  "0" should "be in range" in {
    Util.isNumberInRange("0") should be(true)
  }

  "3600" should "be in range" in {
    Util.isNumberInRange("3600") should be(true)
  }
}
```

Unit tests that need to rely on external dependencies and data service layers should be defined using **mocks**. Mocking is the process of simulating actual behavior. **Mockito, ScalaMock, EasyMock,** and **jMock** are some of the libraries that facilitate mocking.

Dissecting PlaySpecification

The tests written using Specs2 can also be written as follows:

```
class UtilSpec extends PlaySpecification {...}
```

`PlaySpecification` is a trait that provides the required helper methods to test a Play application using Specs2. It is defined as:

```
trait PlaySpecification extends Specification
    with NoTimeConversions
    with PlayRunners
    with HeaderNames
    with Status
    with HttpProtocol
    with DefaultAwaitTimeout
    with ResultExtractors
    with Writeables
    with RouteInvokers
    with FutureAwaits {
}
```

Let's scan through the API exposed by each of these traits to understand its significance:

- `Specification` and `NoTimeConversions` are traits of Specs2. `NoTimeConversions` can be used to deactivate the time conversions.

- `PlayRunners` provides helper methods to execute a block of code in a running application or server with or without specifying the browser.

- `HeaderNames` and `Status` define constants for all the standard HTTP headers and HTTP status codes, respectively, with their relevant names, as shown here:
```
HeaderNames.ACCEPT_CHARSET = "Accept-Charset"
Status.FORBIDDEN = 403
```

    ○ `HttpProtocol` defines the constants related to the HTTP protocol:
```
object HttpProtocol extends HttpProtocol
trait HttpProtocol {
  // Versions
  val HTTP_1_0 = "HTTP/1.0"
```

```
        val HTTP_1_1 = "HTTP/1.1"

        // Other HTTP protocol values
        val CHUNKED = "chunked"
    }
```

○   `ResultExtractors` provides methods to extract data from the HTTP
    response, which is of the `Future[Result]` type. These methods are
    as follows:

   ○   `charset(of: Future[Result])(implicit timeout:`
       `Timeout): Option[String]`

   ○   `contentAsBytes(of: Future[Result])(implicit timeout:`
       `Timeout): Array[Byte]`

   ○   `contentAsJson(of: Future[Result])(implicit timeout:`
       `Timeout): JsValue`

   ○   `contentAsString(of: Future[Result])(implicit timeout:`
       `Timeout): String`

   ○   `contentType(of: Future[Result])(implicit timeout:`
       `Timeout): Option[String]`

   ○   `cookies(of: Future[Result])(implicit timeout:`
       `Timeout): Cookies`

   ○   `flash(of: Future[Result])(implicit timeout: Timeout):`
       `Flash`

   ○   `header(header: String, of: Future[Result])(implicit`
       `timeout: Timeout): Option[String]`

   ○   `headers(of: Future[Result])(implicit timeout:`
       `Timeout): Map[String, String]`

   ○   `redirectLocation(of: Future[Result])(implicit`
       `timeout: Timeout): Option[String]`

   ○   `session(of: Future[Result])(implicit timeout:`
       `Timeout): Session`

   ○   `status(of: Future[Result])(implicit timeout:`
       `Timeout): Int`

The `implicit Timeout` in these method calls is provided by the
`DefaultAwaitTimeout` trait and the default timeout is set to 20 seconds.
This can be overridden by providing an implicit timeout in the scope of
the scenario.

- `RouteInvokers` provides the methods to call a corresponding `Action` for a given request using `Router`. These methods are as follows:

  - `route[T](app: Application, req: Request[T])(implicit w: Writeable[T]): Option[Future[Result]]`

  - `route[T](app: Application, rh: RequestHeader, body: T)(implicit w: Writeable[T]): Option[Future[Result]]`

  - `route[T](req: Request[T])(implicit w: Writeable[T]): Option[Future[Result]]`

  - `route[T](rh: RequestHeader, body: T)(implicit w: Writeable[T]): Option[Future[Result]]`

  - `call[T](action: EssentialAction, rh: RequestHeader, body: T)(implicit w: Writeable[T]): Future[Result]`

  - `call[T](action: EssentialAction, req: FakeRequest[T])(implicit w: Writeable[T]): Future[Result]`

The `implicit Writable` in these method calls is provided by the `Writeables` trait. The `call` methods are inherited from `EssentialActionCaller`.

- The `FutureAwaits` trait provides methods to wait on a request with or without specifying the waiting time.

Although the library that supports ScalaTest for a Play application has an `PlaySpec` abstract class, there is no equivalent to `PlaySpecification` for ScalaTest. Instead, there's a helper object, which is defined as follows:

```
object Helpers extends PlayRunners
    with HeaderNames
    with Status
    with HttpProtocol
    with DefaultAwaitTimeout
    with ResultExtractors
    with Writeables
    with EssentialActionCaller
    with RouteInvokers
    with FutureAwaits
```

PlaySpec is defined as follows:

```
abstract class PlaySpec extends WordSpec with
    MustMatchers with OptionValues with WsScalaTestClient
```

Hence, importing `play.api.test.Helpers` is also sufficient to use only the helper methods.

For the following sections, with regard to tests using Specs2, we will extend PlaySpecification, and for ScalaTest, we will assume that `play.api.test.Helpers` is imported and the test extends to `PlaySpec`.

Unit testing a controller

We might have a simple project with a `User` model and `UserRepo`, defined as follows:

```
case class User(id: Option[Long], loginId: String, name:
  Option[String],
    contactNo: Option[String], dob: Option[Long], address:
      Option[String])

object User{
  implicit val userWrites = Json.writes[User]
}

trait UserRepo {
  def authenticate(loginId: String, password: String): Boolean

  def create(u: User, host: String, password: String):
    Option[Long]

  def update(u: User): Boolean

  def findByLogin(loginId: String): Option[User]

  def delete(userId: Long): Boolean

  def find(userId: Long): Option[User]

  def getAll: Seq[User]

  def updateStatus(userId: Long, isActive: Boolean): Int

  def updatePassword(userId: Long, password: String): Int
}
```

In this project, we need to test a `getUser` method of `UserController`—a controller that is defined to access user details, which are handled by the user model, where `UserController` is defined as follows:

```
object UserController extends Controller {

  /* GET a specific user's details */
```

```
    def getUser(userId: Long) = Action {
      val u = AnormUserRepo.find(userId)
      if (u.isEmpty) {
        NoContent
      }
  else {
        Ok(Json.toJson(u))
      }
    }
  ....
  }
```

AnormUserRepo is an implementation of UserRepo, which uses Anorm for DB transactions. The methods in UserController are mapped in the routes file as follows:

```
GET          /api/user/:userId          controllers.UserController.
getUser(userId:Long)
```

Since mocking Scala objects for tests is not yet fully supported by a testing library, there are different approaches to unit test a controller. These are as follows:

1. Defining all the controller's methods in a trait and then this trait can be extended by an object, while the trait is tested for functionality

2. Defining controllers as classes and wiring up other required services using dependency injection

Both these approaches require us to modify our application code. We can choose the one that suits our coding practices the best. Let's see what these changes are and how to write the corresponding tests in the following sections.

Using traits for controllers

In this approach, we define all the controller's methods in a trait and define the controller by extending this trait. For example, UserController should be defined as follows:

```
trait BaseUserController extends Controller {
this: Controller =>

  val userRepo:UserRepo

  /* GET a specific user's details */
  def getUser(userId: Long) = Action {
    val u = userRepo.find(userId)
```

```
      if (u.isEmpty) {
        NoContent
      } else {
        Ok(Json.toJson(u))
      }
    }
  }

}

  object UserController extends BaseUserController{
    val userRepo = AnormUserRepo
  }
```

Now, we can write tests for the `BaseUserController` trait—`UserControllerSpec` using Specs2 as follows:

```
class UserControllerSpec extends Specification with Mockito {

  "UserController#getUser" should {
    "be valid" in {
      val userRepository = mock[UserRepo]
      val defaultUser = User(Some(1), "loginId", Some("name"),
        Some("contact_no"), Some(20L), Some("address"))
      userRepository.find(1) returns Option(defaultUser)

      class TestController extends Controller with
        BaseUserController{
        val userRepo = userRepository
      }

      val controller = new TestController
      val result: Future[Result] = controller.getUser(1L)
        .apply(FakeRequest())
      val userJson: JsValue = contentAsJson(result)

      userJson should be equalTo(Json.toJson(defaultUser))
    }
  }
}
```

`FakeRequest` is a helper that generates fake HTTP requests while testing.

Here, we mock `UserRepo` and use this mock to generate a new instance of `TestController`. ScalaTest provides integration with Mockito via its `MockitoSugar` trait, so there will be small changes in the code for mocking.

Using ScalaTest, the `UserControllerTest` test will be as follows:

```scala
class UserControllerTest extends PlaySpec with Results with
MockitoSugar {

  "UserController#getUser" should {
    "be valid" in {
      val userRepository = mock[UserRepo]
      val defaultUser = User(Some(1), "loginId", Some("name"),
        Some("contact_no"), Some(20L), Some("address"))
      when(userRepository.find(1)) thenReturn Option(defaultUser)

      class TestController extends Controller with
        BaseUserController{
        val userRepo = userRepository
      }

      val controller = new TestController
      val result: Future[Result] = controller.getUser(1L)
        .apply(FakeRequest())

      val userJson: JsValue = contentAsJson(result)
      userJson mustBe Json.toJson(defaultUser)
    }
  }
}
```

Using dependency injection

We can make our controller depend on specific services, and all of this is configurable through the global object's `getControllerInstance` method by using a dependency injection library.

In this example, we have used **Guice** by adding it as a dependency for our project:

```scala
val appDependencies = Seq(
  ...
  "com.google.inject" % "guice" % "3.0",
  "javax.inject" % "javax.inject" % "1"
)
```

Now, let's update the `getControllerInstance` method in the `Global` object:

```
object Global extends GlobalSettings {

  val injector = Guice.createInjector(new AbstractModule {
    protected def configure() {
      bind(classOf[UserRepo]).to(classOf[AnormUserRepo])
    }
  })

  override def getControllerInstance[A](controllerClass:
    Class[A]): A = injector.getInstance(controllerClass)
}
```

We now define `UserController` as a singleton that extends `play.api.mvc.Controller` and uses `UserRepo`, which is injected:

```
@Singleton
class UserController @Inject()(userRepo: UserRepo) extends Controller
{

  implicit val userWrites = Json.writes[User]

  /* GET a specific user's details */
  def getUser(userId: Long) = Action {
    val u = userRepo.find(userId)
    if (u.isEmpty) {
      NoContent
    }
    else {
      Ok(Json.toJson(u))
    }
  }

}
```

We will also need to modify the routes file:

```
GET        /api/user/:userId        @controllers.UserController.getUser(userId:Long)
```

The @ symbol at the beginning of the method call indicates that the global object's `getControllerInstance` method should be used.

> If we do not add the @ suffix to the method name, it will search for an object with the `UserController` name and throw errors during compilation:
>
> ```
> object UserController is not a member of package
> controllers
> ```
>
> ```
> [error] Note: class UserController exists, but it has
> no companion object.
> ```
>
> ```
> [error] GET          /api/user/:userId
> controllers.UserController.getUser(userId:Long)
> ```

Finally, we can write a unit test using Specs2 as follows:

```scala
class UserControllerSpec extends Specification with Mockito {

  "UserController#getUser" should {
    "be valid" in {
      val userRepository = mock[AnormUserRepo]
      val defaultUser = User(Some(1), "loginId", Some("name"),
        Some("contact_no"), Some(20L), Some("address"))
      userRepository.find(1) returns Option(defaultUser)

      val controller = new UserController(userRepository)
      val result: Future[Result] = controller.getUser(1L)
        .apply(FakeRequest())
      val userJson: JsValue = contentAsJson(result)

      userJson should be equalTo(Json.toJson(defaultUser))
    }
  }
}
```

Here, we mock `AnormUserRepo` and use this mock to generate a new instance of `UserController`.

The same test using ScalaTest will be as follows:

```scala
class UserControllerTest extends PlaySpec with Results with
MockitoSugar {

  "UserController#getUser" should {
    "be valid" in {
      val userRepository = mock[AnormUserRepo]
      val defaultUser = User(Some(1), "loginId", Some("name"),
        Some("contact_no"), Some(20L), Some("address"))
```

```
    when(userRepository.find(1)) thenReturn Option(defaultUser)

    val controller = new UserController(userRepository)
    val result: Future[Result] = controller.getUser(1L)
      .apply(FakeRequest())
    val userJson: JsValue = contentAsJson(result)

    userJson mustBe Json.toJson(defaultUser)
    }
  }
}
```

The following table summarizes the key differences in both these approaches, so that it's easier to decide which one suits your requirement in the best way:

Using traits for controllers	Using dependency injection
It requires defining and not just declaring all the methods to be supported by a controller in a trait.	It requires a controller to be defined as a singleton class and provides implementations for the global object's `getControllerInstance` method.
It does not require additional libraries.	It requires using a dependency injection library and provides flexibility to plug-in different classes in different application modes.
It requires defining an additional class for a controller, which extends a trait for testing.	It does not require any additional class definitions to test a controller, since a new instance can be instantiated from a singleton.

For more examples on dependency injection, refer to `https://www.playframework.com/documentation/2.3.x/ScalaDependencyInjection`.

Functional testing

Let's look at some of Play's test cases to see how to use the helper methods. For example, consider the `DevErrorPageSpec` test, which is defined as follows:

```
object DevErrorPageSpec extends PlaySpecification{

  "devError.scala.html" should {

    val testExceptionSource = new
      play.api.PlayException.ExceptionSource
      ("test", "making sure the link shows up") {
```

```
      . . .
    }
    ....
    "show prod error page in prod mode" in {
      val fakeApplication = new FakeApplication() {
        override val mode = play.api.Mode.Prod
      }
      running(fakeApplication) {
        val result = DefaultGlobal.onError(FakeRequest(),
          testExceptionSource)
        Helpers.contentAsString(result) must contain("Oops, an
          error occurred")
      }
    }
  }
}
```

This test starts `FakeApplication` with the Prod mode and checks the response when `FakeRequest` encounters an exception.

`FakeApplication` extends an application and is defined as follows:

```
case class FakeApplication(config: Map[String, Any] = Map(),
                           path: File = new File("."),
                           sources: Option[SourceMapper] = None,
                           mode: Mode.Mode = Mode.Test,
                           global: GlobalSettings = DefaultGlobal,
                           plugins: Seq[Plugin] = Nil) extends
Application {
  val classloader = Thread.currentThread.getContextClassLoader
  lazy val configuration = Configuration.from(config)
}
```

The method that is running is part of PlayRunners and executes a block of code in the context of a given application. It is defined as follows:

```
def running[T](app: Application)(block: => T): T = {
    synchronized {
      try {
        Play.start(app)
        block
      } finally {
        Play.stop()
      }
    }
}
```

PlayRunners has a few more definitions of how to run, these are:

- `running[T](testServer: TestServer)(block: => T): T`: This can be used to execute a block of code in a running server.

- `running[T](testServer: TestServer, webDriver: WebDriver)(block: TestBrowser => T): T`: This can be used to execute a block of code in a running server with a test browser.

- `running[T, WEBDRIVER <: WebDriver](testServer: TestServer, webDriver: Class[WEBDRIVER])(block: TestBrowser => T): T`: This can also be used to execute a block of code in a running server with a test browser using Selenium WebDriver. This method uses the previous method internally.

Instead of using the `running` method directly, as an alternative, we could define our tests using the wrapper classes, which make use of the running. There are different helpers for Specs2 and ScalaTest.

Using Specs2

First, let's look at the ones available when using Specs2. They are as follows:

- `WithApplication`: It is used to execute a test within the context of a running application. For example, consider a situation where we want to write functional tests for `CountController`, which is responsible for getting a count of distinct data grouped by a perspective. We can write the test as follows:

```
class CountControllerSpec extends PlaySpecification with
BeforeExample {

  override def before: Any = {
    TestHelper.clearDB
  }

  """Counter query""" should {
    """fetch count of visits grouped by browser names""" in new
WithApplication {
      TestHelper.postSampleData

      val queryString = """applicationId=39&perspective=
        browser&from=1389949200000&till=
        1399145400000""".stripMargin

      val request = FakeRequest(GET, "/query/count?" +
        queryString)
```

```
      val response = route(request)
      val result = response.get
      status(result) must equalTo(OK)
      contentAsJson(result) must
        equalTo(TestHelper.browserCount)
  }
}
```

Here, assume that `TestHelper` is a helper object specifically defined for simplifying the code of test cases (extracting common processes as methods).

If we need to specify `FakeApplication`, we can do so by passing it as an argument to the `WithApplication` constructor:

```
val app = FakeApplication()
  """fetch count of visits grouped by browser names""" in new
WithApplication(app) {
```

This comes in handy when we want to change the default application configurations, GlobalSettings, and so on for the tests.

- `WithServer`: It is used to execute tests within the context of a running application on a new `TestServer`. This is quite useful when we need to start our `FakeApplication` on a new `TestServer` at a specific port. After slightly modifying the previous example:

```
  """fetch count of visits grouped by browser names""" in new
WithServer(app = app, port = testPort) {
  {
      ...
  }
}
```

- `WithBrowser`: It is used to test an application's functionality by performing certain actions in browsers. For example, consider a dummy application where the page title changes on the click of a button. We can test it as follows:

```
class AppSpec extends PlaySpecification {
  val app: FakeApplication =
    FakeApplication(
      withRoutes = TestRoute
    )

    "run in firefox" in new WithBrowser(webDriver =
      WebDriverFactory(FIREFOX), app = app) {
    browser.goTo("/testing")
```

```
browser.$("#title").getTexts().get(0) must
  equalTo("Test Page")

browser.$("b").click()

browser.$("#title").getTexts().get(0) must
  equalTo("testing")
}}
```

We are assuming TestRoute is a partial function that maps to some of the routes which can then be used in tests.

Using ScalaTest

Now, lets see what **ScalaTestPlus-Play**, the library with helper methods that are used for testing with the help of ScalaTest, has to offer. In this section, we will see examples from ScalatestPlus-Play wherever applicable. The helpers for ScalaTest are as follows:

- OneAppPerSuite: It starts FakeApplication using Play.start before running any tests in a suite and then stops it once they are completed. The application is exposed through the variable app and can be overridden if required. From ExampleSpec.scala:

```scala
class ExampleSpec extends PlaySpec with OneAppPerSuite {

  // Override app if you need a FakeApplication with other than
non-default parameters.
  implicit override lazy val app: FakeApplication =
    FakeApplication(additionalConfiguration =
      Map("ehcacheplugin" -> "disabled"))

  "The OneAppPerSuite trait" must {
    "provide a FakeApplication" in {
      app.configuration.getString("ehcacheplugin") mustBe
        Some("disabled")
    }
    "make the FakeApplication available implicitly" in {
      def getConfig(key: String)(implicit app: Application)
        = app.configuration.getString(key)
      getConfig("ehcacheplugin") mustBe Some("disabled")
    }
    "start the FakeApplication" in {
      Play.maybeApplication mustBe Some(app)
    }
  }
}
```

If we wish to use the same application for all or multiple suites, we can define a nested suite. For such an example, we can refer to `NestedExampleSpec.scala` from the library.

- `OneAppPerTest`: It starts a new `FakeApplication` for each test defined in the suite. The application is exposed through the `newAppForTest` method and can be overridden if required. For example, consider the `OneAppTest` test, where each test uses a different `FakeApplication` obtained through `newAppForTest`:

```scala
class DiffAppTest extends UnitSpec with OneAppPerTest {

  private val colors = Seq("red", "blue", "yellow")

  private var colorCode = 0

  override def newAppForTest(testData: TestData):
    FakeApplication = {
    val currentCode = colorCode
    colorCode+=1
    FakeApplication(additionalConfiguration = Map("foo" ->
      "bar",
      "ehcacheplugin" -> "disabled",
      "color" -> colors(currentCode)
    ))
  }

  def getConfig(key: String)(implicit app: Application) =
    app.configuration.getString(key)

  "The OneAppPerTest trait" must {
    "provide a FakeApplication" in {
      app.configuration.getString("color") mustBe
        Some("red")
    }
    "make another FakeApplication available implicitly" in {
      getConfig("color") mustBe Some("blue")
    }
    "make the third FakeApplication available implicitly"
      in {
      getConfig("color") mustBe Some("yellow")
    }
  }
}
```

- OneServerPerSuite: It starts a new FakeApplication and a new TestServer for the suite. The application is exposed through the variable app and can be overridden if required. The server's port is set from the variable port and can be changed/modified if required. This has been demonstrated in the example for OneServerPerSuite (ExampleSpec2.scala):

```scala
class ExampleSpec extends PlaySpec with OneServerPerSuite {

  // Override app if you need a FakeApplication with other than
  non-default parameters.
    implicit override lazy val app: FakeApplication =
      FakeApplication(additionalConfiguration =
        Map("ehcacheplugin" -> "disabled"))

  "The OneServerPerSuite trait" must {
    "provide a FakeApplication" in {
      app.configuration.getString("ehcacheplugin") mustBe
        Some("disabled")
    }
    "make the FakeApplication available implicitly" in {
      def getConfig(key: String)(implicit app: Application)
        = app.configuration.getString(key)
      getConfig("ehcacheplugin") mustBe Some("disabled")
    }
    "start the FakeApplication" in {
      Play.maybeApplication mustBe Some(app)
    }
    "provide the port number" in {
      port mustBe Helpers.testServerPort
    }
    "provide an actual running server" in {
      import java.net._
      val url = new URL("http://localhost:" + port +
        "/boum")
      val con = url.openConnection()
        .asInstanceOf[HttpURLConnection]
      try con.getResponseCode mustBe 404
      finally con.disconnect()
    }
  }
}
```

When we require multiple suites to use the same FakeApplication and TestServer, we can define tests using a nested suite similar to NestedExampleSpec2.scala.

- OneServerPerTest: It starts a new FakeApplication and TestServer for each test defined in the suite. The application is exposed through the newAppForTest method and can be overridden if required. For example, consider the DiffServerTest test, where each test uses a different FakeApplication obtained through newAppForTest and the TestServer port is overridden:

```
class DiffServerTest extends PlaySpec with OneServerPerTest {

  private val colors = Seq("red", "blue", "yellow")

  private var code = 0

  override def newAppForTest(testData: TestData):
FakeApplication = {
    val currentCode = code
    code += 1
    FakeApplication(additionalConfiguration = Map("foo" ->
      "bar",
      "ehcacheplugin" -> "disabled",
      "color" -> colors(currentCode)
    ))
  }

  override lazy val port = 1234

  def getConfig(key: String)(implicit app: Application) =
    app.configuration.getString(key)

  "The OneServerPerTest trait" must {
    "provide a FakeApplication" in {
      app.configuration.getString("color") mustBe
        Some("red")
    }
    "make another FakeApplication available implicitly" in {
      getConfig("color") mustBe Some("blue")
    }
    "start server at specified port" in {
      port mustBe 1234
    }
  }
}
```

- OneBrowserPerSuite: It provides a new Selenium WebDriver instance per suite. For example, assume that we wish to test the clicking of a button by opening the application in Firefox, the test can be written in the same way as ExampleSpec3.scala:

```scala
@FirefoxBrowser
class ExampleSpec extends PlaySpec with OneServerPerSuite with
OneBrowserPerSuite with FirefoxFactory {

  // Override app if you need a FakeApplication with other than
non-default parameters.
  implicit override lazy val app: FakeApplication =
    FakeApplication(
      additionalConfiguration = Map("ehcacheplugin" ->
        "disabled"),
      withRoutes = TestRoute
    )

  "The OneBrowserPerSuite trait" must {
    "provide a FakeApplication" in {
      app.configuration.getString("ehcacheplugin") mustBe
        Some("disabled")
    }
    "make the FakeApplication available implicitly" in {
      def getConfig(key: String)(implicit app: Application)
        = app.configuration.getString(key)
      getConfig("ehcacheplugin") mustBe Some("disabled")
    }
    "provide a web driver" in {
      go to ("http://localhost:" + port + "/testing")
      pageTitle mustBe "Test Page"
      click on find(name("b")).value
      eventually { pageTitle mustBe "scalatest" }
    }
  }
}
```

We are assuming TestRoute is a partial function that maps to some of the routes, which can then be used in tests.

The same trait can be used to test the application within multiple browsers, as demonstrated in `MultiBrowserExampleSpec.scala`. To execute tests in all the browsers, we should use `AllBrowsersPerSuite`, as follows:

```
class AllBrowsersPerSuiteTest extends PlaySpec with
OneServerPerSuite with AllBrowsersPerSuite {

  // Override newAppForTest if you need a FakeApplication with
other than non-default parameters.
  override lazy val app: FakeApplication =
    FakeApplication(
      withRoutes = TestRoute
    )

  // Place tests you want run in different browsers in the
`sharedTests` method:
  def sharedTests(browser: BrowserInfo) = {

      "navigate to testing "+browser.name in {
        go to ("http://localhost:" + port + "/testing")
        pageTitle mustBe "Test Page"
        click on find(name("b")).value
        eventually { pageTitle mustBe "testing" }
      }

      "navigate to hello in a new window"+browser.name in {
        go to ("http://localhost:" + port + "/hello")
        pageTitle mustBe "Hello"
        click on find(name("b")).value
        eventually { pageTitle mustBe "helloUser" }
      }
  }

  // Place tests you want run just once outside the `sharedTests`
method
  // in the constructor, the usual place for tests in a `PlaySpec`

  "The test" must {
    "start the FakeApplication" in {
      Play.maybeApplication mustBe Some(app)
    }
  }
}
```

The trait `OneBrowserPerSuite` can also be used with nested tests. Refer to `NestedExampleSpec3.scala`.

- `OneBrowserPerTest`: It starts a new browser session for each test in the suite. This can be noticed by running the `ExampleSpec4.scala` test. It's similar to `ExampleSpec3.scala`, but `OneServerPerSuite` and `OneBrowserPerSuite` have been replaced with `OneServerPerTest` and `OneBrowserPerTest`, respectively, as shown here:

```
@FirefoxBrowser
class ExampleSpec extends PlaySpec with OneServerPerTest with
OneBrowserPerTest with FirefoxFactory {

  ...

}
```

We've also replaced the overridden app variable with the `newAppForTest` overridden method. Try writing a test that uses the `AllBrowsersPerTest` trait.

 You can run into an InvalidActorNameException when running multiple functional tests simultaneously on an application, which defines custom actors. We can avoid this by defining a nested test where multiple tests use the same `FakeApplication`.

Summary

In this chapter, we saw how a Play application can be tested using Specs2 or ScalaTest. We have also come across the different helper methods available to simplify testing a Play application. In the unit testing section, we discussed the different approaches that can be taken while designing models and controller based on the preferred testing process using traits with defined methods or dependency injection. We also discussed the functional testing of a Play application within the context of an application with a test server and within a browser using Selenium WebDrivers.

In the next chapter, we will discuss debugging and logging in to your Play application.

10
Debugging and Logging

Debugging and logging are the tools that a developer can use to identify the root cause of bugs or unexpected behavior of applications.

The aim of debugging is to find a defect or pain point in our code, which is responsible for a problem. Logging gives us information about an application's state and the various stages of processing it. In this chapter, we will cover the following topics:

- Debugging a Play application
- Configuring logging
- Experimenting in a Scala console

Debugging a Play application

Play applications can be debugged using a **Java Platform Debugger Architecture (JPDA)** transport. According to the Oracle documentation (refer to `http://docs.oracle.com/javase/7/docs/technotes/guides/jpda/conninv.html`):

A JPDA Transport is a method of communication between a debugger and the virtual machine that is being debugged (hereafter the target VM). The communication is connection oriented - one side acts as a server, listening for a connection. The other side acts as a client and connects to the server. JPDA allows either the debugger application or the target VM to act as the server.

We can start a console in debug mode with any one of the following commands:

- By using `play`:

  ```
  play debug
  ```

- By using `activator`:

  ```
  activator -jvm-debug <port>
  ```

- By using `sbt`:

  ```
  sbt -jvm-debug <port>
  ```

All these commands are just wrappers used to start the target VM in debug mode through the invocation options:

```
-Xdebug -Xrunjdwp:transport=dt_socket,server=y,suspend=n,address=<port>
```

> The `play` command uses the `JPDA_PORT` or `9999` environment variable for the port variable. After setting `JPDA_PORT` to the desired port, the target VM will listen to that port.

Configuring an IDE for debugging

Once we start the console in debug mode, we can connect our IDE and debug the application when it's running. If you are familiar with how this can be done, you can skip this section.

The process of configuring the IDE will be similar to the one used in all the IDEs. Let's see how it's done in **IntelliJ Idea** through the following steps:

1. Select **Edit Configurations…** from the the **Run** menu. A dialog will pop up. It will be similar to the following screenshot:

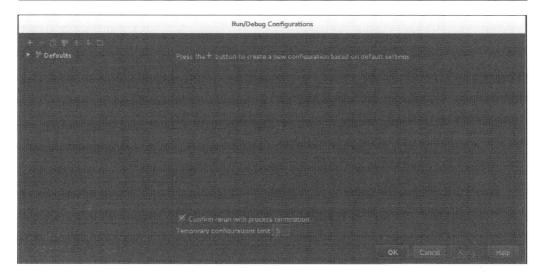

2. Click on **+** and a menu similar to this screenshot will be visible:

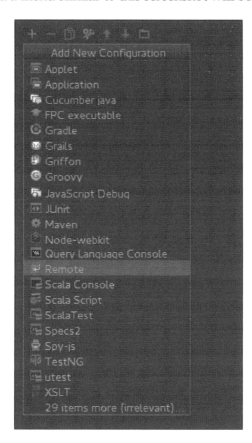

3. Select **Remote** and update the **Name** and **Port** fields:

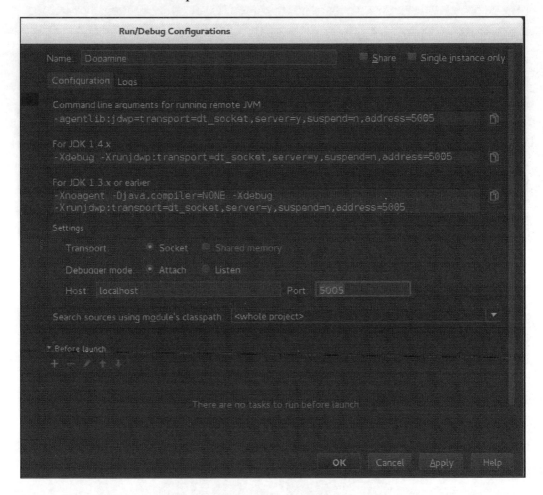

4. After this, click on the green bug, which is now visible at the top-right corner of the IDE, and we are ready to start debugging the application:

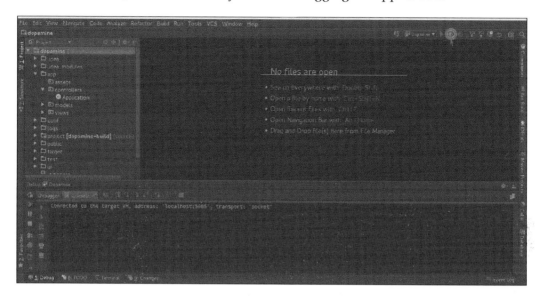

Experimenting in a Scala console

A Scala console is very handy when you're working on a Scala project. The same console is available in our Play application's console as well. All that we need to do to get the Scala console is execute the `console` command in our application console:

```
[app]$ console

[info] Compiling 3 Scala sources to /home/app/target/scala-2.10/
classes...

[info] Starting scala interpreter...

[info]

Welcome to Scala version 2.10.4 (Java HotSpot(TM) 64-Bit Server VM, Java
1.7.0_60).

Type in expressions to have them evaluated.

Type :help for more information.


scala>
```

However, we can only call methods from **models** or **utils**. If classes or objects within these packages utilize `Play.application.configuration` or attempt to fetch data from the DB or some other Play utils, we will not be able to instantiate them. This is because most of the Play components require access to an instance of the currently running Play application. Importing `play.api.Play.current` makes this possible but not entirely; we still need a running application, which will be marked as the current application.

Let's create an application and start it from the Scala console, and then import `play.api.Play.current`:

```
scala> :pas
// Entering paste mode (ctrl-D to finish)


import play.api.Play


val application = new DefaultApplication(new java.io.File("."), this.
getClass.getClassLoader, None, Mode.Dev)
Play.start(application)


import play.api.Play.current
```

Once we exit paste mode, the code will be interpreted and the application will be started. We can see this from this output:

```
// Exiting paste mode, now interpreting.


SLF4J: Class path contains multiple SLF4J bindings.
SLF4J: Found binding in [jar:file:/home/.ivy2/cache/ch.qos.logback/
logback-classic/jars/logback-classic-1.1.1.jar!/org/slf4j/impl/
StaticLoggerBinder.class]
SLF4J: Found binding in [jar:file:/home/.ivy2/cache/org.slf4j/slf4j-
log4j12/jars/slf4j-log4j12-1.7.2.jar!/org/slf4j/impl/StaticLoggerBinder.
class]
SLF4J: See http://www.slf4j.org/codes.html#multiple_bindings for an
explanation.
SLF4J: Actual binding is of type [ch.qos.logback.classic.util.
ContextSelectorStaticBinder]
[info] play - Application started (Dev)
import play.api.Play
application: play.api.DefaultApplication =
  play.api.DefaultApplication@29600952
```

```
import play.api.Play.current


scala>
```

Now, we can view the configuration, view or modify data, and so on. For example, let's try to get the application's configuration:

```
scala> Play.application.configuration
res7: play.api.Configuration = Configuration(Config(SimpleConfigOb
ject({"akka":{"actor":{"creation-timeout":"20s","debug":{"autorec
eive":"off","event-stream":"off","fsm":"off","lifecycle":"off","r
eceive":"off","router-misconfiguration":"off","unhandled":"off"},
"default-dispatcher":{"attempt-teamwork":"on","default-executor":-
{"fallback":"fork-join-executor"},"executor":"default-executor","fork-
join-executor":{"parallelism-factor":3,"parallelism-max":64,"parallelism-
min":8},"mailbox-requirement":"","shutdown-timeout":"1s","thread-pool-
executor":{"allow-core-timeout":"on","core-pool-size-factor":3,"core-
pool-size-max":64,"core-pool-size-min":8,"keep-alive-time":"60s","max-
pool-size-factor":3,"max-pool-size-max":64,"max-pool-size-min":8,"task-
queue-size":-1,"task-queue-type":"linked"},"thro...
```

Nice, isn't it? Yet, this is not enough if we want to call actions and check results for different inputs. For such cases, we shouldn't use the `console` command, but instead, the `test:console` command:

```
[app] $ test:console
[info] Starting scala interpreter...
[info]
Welcome to Scala version 2.10.4 (Java HotSpot(TM) 64-Bit Server VM, Java
1.7.0_60).
Type in expressions to have them evaluated.
Type :help for more information.


scala> :pas
// Entering paste mode (ctrl-D to finish)

import play.api.test.Helpers._
import play.api.test._
import play.api.Play

val application = FakeApplication()
```

```
Play.start(application)

import play.api.Play.current
// Exiting paste mode, now interpreting.
...
```

Now, from this Scala console, we can view the configuration, modify data, as well as call an action:

```
scala> Play.application.configuration
res0: play.api.Configuration = Configuration(Config(SimpleConfigOb
ject({"akka":{"actor":{"creation-timeout":"20s","debug":{"autorec
eive":"off","event-stream":"off","fsm":"off","lifecycle":"off","r
eceive":"off","router-misconfiguration":"off","unhandled":"off"},
"default-dispatcher":{"attempt-teamwork":"on","default-executor":-
{"fallback":"fork-join-executor"},"executor":"default-executor","fork-
join-executor":{"parallelism-factor":3,"parallelism-max":64,"parallelism-
min":8},"mailbox-requirement":"","shutdown-timeout":"1s","thread-pool-
executor":{"allow-core-timeout":"on","core-pool-size-factor":3,"core-
pool-size-max":64,"core-pool-size-min":8,"keep-alive-time":"60s","max-
pool-size-factor":3,"max-pool-size-max":64,"max-pool-size-min":8,"task-
queue-size":-1,"task-queue-type":"linked"},"thro...
```

```
scala> controllers.Application.index("John").apply(FakeRequest())
res1: scala.concurrent.Future[play.api.mvc.Result] = scala.concurrent.
impl.Promise$KeptPromise@6fbd57ac
```

```
scala> contentAsString(res1)
res2: String = Hello John
```

 Use test:console instead of console; you need not switch when you decide to check an action.

Logging

Logging is the act of recording data about when and why an event occurred for an application. Logs are extremely useful if they've been handled correctly; otherwise, they are just noise. By reviewing the log output, there is a good chance that you can determine the cause of an event.

Logs are useful not just to handle application errors, but also to protect an application from misuse and malicious attacks as well as understand different aspects of a business.

Play's logging API

Play exposes the logging API through `play.api.Logger`. Let's have a look at the class and object definition of it:

```
class Logger(val logger: Slf4jLogger) extends LoggerLike

object Logger extends LoggerLike {

  ...
  val logger = LoggerFactory.getLogger("application")

  def apply(name: String): Logger = new
    Logger(LoggerFactory.getLogger(name))

  def apply[T](clazz: Class[T]): Logger = new
    Logger(LoggerFactory.getLogger(clazz))

  ...

}
```

The `LoggerLike` trait is just a wrapper over `Slf4jLogger`. By default, all application logs are mapped to `Logger` with the application name and the Play-related logs are mapped to `Logger` with the Play name.

After importing `play.api.Logger`, we can use the default logger or define a custom one in these ways:

- By using a default logger:

```
import play.api.Logger
object Task{
  def delete(id:Long) = {
    logger.debug(s"deleting task with id $id")
    ...
  }
}
```

- By using a logger with its class name:

```
import play.api.Logger
object Task{
  private lazy val taskLogger = Logger(getClass)
  def delete(id:Long) = {
    taskLogger.debug(s"deleting task with id $id")
    ...
  }
}
```

- By using a logger with its custom name:

```
import play.api.Logger
object Task{
  private lazy val taskLogger = Logger("application.model")
  def delete(id:Long) = {
    taskLogger.debug(s"deleting task with id $id")
    ...
  }
}
```

 The methods supported by `Logger` are documented in the API at https://www.playframework.com/documentation/2.3.x/api/scala/index.html#play.api.Logger.

Log configuration in Play

The Play Framework uses `Logback` as the logging engine. The default configuration is as follows:

```
<configuration>

  <conversionRule conversionWord="coloredLevel"
    converterClass="play.api.Logger$ColoredLevel" />

  <appender name="FILE" class="ch.qos.logback.core.FileAppender">
    <file>${application.home}/logs/application.log</file>
    <encoder>
      <pattern>%date - [%level] - from %logger in %thread
        %n%message%n%xException%n</pattern>
    </encoder>
  </appender>

  <appender name="STDOUT" class="ch.qos.logback.core.ConsoleAppender">
```

```
    <encoder>
      <pattern>%coloredLevel %logger{15} -
        %message%n%xException{5}</pattern>
    </encoder>
  </appender>

  <logger name="play" level="INFO" />
  <logger name="application" level="DEBUG" />

  <!-- Off these ones as they are annoying, and anyway we manage
    configuration ourself -->
  <logger name="com.avaje.ebean.config.PropertyMapLoader"
    level="OFF" />
  <logger
    name="com.avaje.ebeaninternal.server.core.XmlConfigLoader"
      level="OFF" />
  <logger
    name="com.avaje.ebeaninternal.server.lib.BackgroundThread"
      level="OFF" />
  <logger name="com.gargoylesoftware.htmlunit.javascript"
    level="OFF" />

  <root level="ERROR">
    <appender-ref ref="STDOUT" />
    <appender-ref ref="FILE" />
  </root>

</configuration>
```

This configuration writes logs in `projectHome/logs/application.log`. Due to this, one huge file is generated. We could modify this configuration by providing a custom `logger.xml`.

The custom log file configuration can be set in two ways:

- By saving the configuration in `conf/application-logger.xml` or `conf/logger.xml`. Although using any one of the filenames, such as `application-logger.xml` or `logger.xml`, works when both are present, the settings of `logger.xml` are not applied.

- By specifying the file via a system property. This method has a higher precedence over the other option.

There are three properties:

- `logger.resource`: This property sets a file within the class path
- `logger.file`: This property sets a file through its absolute path
- `logger.url`: This property sets a file using a URL in this way:

```
[app]$ start -Dlogger.url=http://serverPath/conf/appName/logger.
xml
```

Another important aspect of configuring logging is by setting the desired log level. We will discuss this in the next section.

Log levels

Log levels can be set in `conf/application.conf`. The default values are as follows:

```
# Root logger:
logger.root=ERROR

# Logger used by the framework:
logger.play=INFO

# Logger provided to your application:
logger.application=DEBUG
```

We can also set the log levels for the classes belonging to specific packages and third-party libraries in this way:

```
logger.com.apache.cassandra = DEBUG
```

The supported log levels in the decreasing order of severity are as follows:

- ERROR
- WARN
- INFO
- DEBUG
- TRACE

If we wish to turn off logging for some classes or packages, we can set the log level as OFF. This will disable logging for a particular logger.

Some libraries have transitive dependencies on logging libraries. It is best to exclude these logging packages when defining a dependency. It can be done as follows:

```
"orgName" % "packageName" % "version" excludeAll(
    ExclusionRule(organization = "org.slf4j"),
    ExclusionRule(organization = "ch.qos.logback"))
```

Summary

In this chapter, we discussed how to configure the debugging of a Play application in the IDE. We also covered how to start a Play application in a Scala console. This chapter also covered the logging API provided by the Play Framework and customizing the log format.

A lot of web applications make use of the third-party APIs either to avoid rewriting the existing code or to make it easy for users to adopt their applications. In the next chapter, we will be checking out how developers can use existing external APIs in a Play application.

11
Web Services and Authentication

The internet is vast and constantly expanding. A lot of day-to-day tasks can be dealt with in a simpler manner—bill payments, checking reviews of a product, booking movie tickets, and so on. In addition to this, most electronic devices can now be connected to the Internet, such as mobile phones, watches, surveillance systems, and security systems. These can communicate with each other and they need not all be of the same brand. Applications can utilize user-specific information and provide features with better customization. Most importantly, we can decide if we wish to share our information with the application by authenticating it or not.

In this chapter, we will cover Play Framework's support for the following:

- Calling web services
- OpenID and OAuth authentication

Calling web services

Suppose we need to book a flight ticket online. We can do this by using either the website of the flight's brand (such as Lufthansa, Emirates, and so on), or a travel booking website (such as ClearTrip, MakeMyTrip, and so on). How is it that we can do the same task from two or more different websites?

The website of the flight's brand provides some APIs with which the travel booking websites work. These API can be freely available or charged by a contract, which is for the provider and the other third-party involved to decide. These APIs are also called web services.

A web service is more or less a method that is called over the Internet. Only the provider is fully aware of the internal working of these sites. Those who use the web service are only aware of the purpose and its possible outcome.

Many applications require/prefer to use third-party APIs to complete common tasks for various reasons, such as common norms in the business domain, easier means to provide secure authorization, or to avoid the overhead of maintenance, and so on.

The Play Framework has a web service API specifically to meet such requirements. The web service API can be used by including it as a dependency:

```
libraryDependencies ++= Seq(
  ws
)
```

A common use case is to send an e-mail with the link for account verification and/or resetting the password using a transactional e-mail API service, such as Mailgun, SendGrid, and so on.

Let's assume that our application has such a requirement, and we have an `Email` object that handles all these kind of transactions. We need one method to send e-mails that makes actual calls to the e-mailing API service, and then other methods that internally call send. Using the Play web service API, we could define `Email` as:

```
object Email {

  val logger = Logger(getClass)

  private def send(emailIds: Seq[String], subject: String, content:
    String): Unit = {

    var properties: Properties = new Properties()

    try {

      properties.load(new FileInputStream("/opt/appName/mail-config.
properties"))

      val url: String = properties.getProperty("url")

      val apiKey: String = properties.getProperty("api")

      val from: String = properties.getProperty("from")

      val requestHolder: WSRequestHolder = WS.url(url).withAuth("api",
apiKey, WSAuthScheme.BASIC)
```

```
val requestData = Map(

  "from" -> Seq(from),

  "to" -> emailIds,

  "subject" -> Seq(subject),

  "text" -> Seq(content))

val response: Future[WSResponse] = requestHolder.
  post(requestData)

response.map(

  res => {

    val responseMsg: String = res.json.toString()

    if (res.status == 200) {

      logger.info(responseMsg)

    } else {

      logger.error(responseMsg)

    }

  }

)

} catch {

case exp: IOException =>

  logger.error("Failed to load email configuration properties.")

}

}
```

```scala
def sendVerification(userId: Long, emailId: String, host: String):
  Unit = {

  val subject: String = "Email Verification"

  val content: String =

    s"""To verify your account on <appName>, please click on the
link below

       |

       |http://$host/validate/user/$userId""".stripMargin

  send(Seq(emailId), subject, content)

}

def recoverPassword(emailId: String, password: String): Unit = {

  val subject: String = "Password Recovery"

  val emailContent: String = s"Your password has been reset.The new
password is $password"

  send(Seq(emailId), subject, emailContent)

}

}
```

The web service API is exposed through the `WS` object, which provides methods to query web services as an HTTP client. In the preceding code snippet, we have used the web service API to make a post request. Other available methods to trigger a request and fetch a response or response stream are:

- `get` or `getStream`
- `put` or `putAndRetrieveStream`
- `post` or `postAndRetrieveStream`
- `delete`
- `head`

The result of any of these calls is of the `Future[WSResponse]` type, so we can safely say that the web service API is asynchronous.

It is not restricted to REST services. For example, let's say we use a SOAP service to fetch the currencies of all countries:

```
def displayCurrency = Action.async {

  val url: String = "http://www.webservicex.net/country.asmx"

  val wsReq: String = """<?xml version="1.0" encoding="utf-8"?>

                        |<soap12:Envelope xmlns:xsi="http://www.
  w3.org/2001/XMLSchema-instance" xmlns:xsd="http://www.w3.org/2001/
  XMLSchema" xmlns:soap12="http://www.w3.org/2003/05/soap-envelope">

                        |  <soap12:Body>

                        |    <GetCurrencies xmlns="http://www.
  webserviceX.NET" />

                        |  </soap12:Body>

                        |</soap12:Envelope>""".stripMargin

  val response: Future[WSResponse] = WS.url(url).
  withHeaders("Content-Type" -> "application/soap+xml").post(wsReq)

  response map {

    data => Ok(data.xml)

  }

}
```

An HTTP request can be built using `WS.url()`, which returns an instance of `WSRequestHolder`. The `WSRequestHolder` trait has methods to add headers, authentication, request parameters, data, and so on. Here is another example of commonly used methods:

```
WS.url("http://third-party.com/service?=serviceName")
.withAuth("api","apiKey", WSAuthScheme.BASIC)
.withQueryString("month" -> "12",
        "year" -> "2014",
        "code" -> "code")
.withHeaders(HeaderNames.ACCEPT -> MimeTypes.JSON)
.get
```

Although in this example we have used Basic authentication, the web service API supports most of the commonly used authentication schemes, which you can find at the following links:

- **Basic**: http://en.wikipedia.org/wiki/Basic_access_authentication
- **Digest**: http://en.wikipedia.org/wiki/Digest_access_authentication
- **Simple and Protected GSSAPI Negotiation Mechanism (SPNEGO)**: http://en.wikipedia.org/wiki/SPNEGO
- **NT LAN Manager (NTLM)**: http://en.wikipedia.org/wiki/NT_LAN_Manager
- **Kerberos**: http://en.wikipedia.org/wiki/Kerberos_(protocol)

All the methods available through the `ws` object simply call the relevant methods of the available `WSAPI` trait's implementation. The web service API provided by default utilizes Ning's AysncHttpClient (refer to https://github.com/AsyncHttpClient/async-http-client). If we wish to use any other HTTP client, we need to implement the `WSAPI` trait and bind it through a plugin. When we add the `ws` Play library, it adds `play.api.libs.ws.ning.NingWSPlugin` to our application, which is defined as:

```
class NingWSPlugin(app: Application) extends WSPlugin {

  @volatile var loaded = false

  override lazy val enabled = true

  private val config = new DefaultWSConfigParser(app.configuration,
    app.classloader).parse()

  private lazy val ningAPI = new NingWSAPI(app, config)

  override def onStart() {
    loaded = true
  }

  override def onStop() {
    if (loaded) {
      ningAPI.resetClient()
      loaded = false
    }
  }

  def api = ningAPI

}
```

In a Play app, using SSL with WS requires a few changes in the configuration, and it is documented at `https://www.playframework.com/documentation/2.3.x/WsSSL`.

Since a huge number of applications rely on a user's data from various sources, Play provides an API for OpenID and OAuth. We will discuss these in the following sections.

OpenID

OpenID is an authentication protocol, wherein OpenID Providers validate the identity of a user for third-party applications. An OpenID Provider is any service/application that provides an OpenID to users. Yahoo, AOL, and others are a few examples of these. Applications that require a user's OpenID to complete transactions are known as OpenID Consumers.

The flow of control in an OpenID Consumer is as follows:

1. The user is directed to the login page of the supported/selected OpenID Provider.

2. Once the user completes logging in, the OpenID Provider informs the user about user-related data requested by the OpenID Consumer.

3. If the user agrees to share the information, he or she is redirected to the page requested by him or her on the consumer application. The information is added to the request URL. The information is termed as attribute properties and this is documented at `http://openid.net/specs/openid-attribute-properties-list-1_0-01.html`.

Play provides an API to simplify OpenID transactions, which is documented at `https://www.playframework.com/documentation/2.3.x/api/scala/index.html#play.api.libs.openid.OpenID$`.

Two critical methods are as follows:

- `redirectURL`: This is used for verifying the user, requesting specific user information and redirecting it to the callback page

- `verifiedId`: This is used to extract user information from a verified OpenID callback request

Let's build an application that uses OpenID from the provider, Yahoo. We can define the controller as follows:

```scala
object Application extends Controller {

  def index = Action.async {

    implicit request =>

      OpenID.verifiedId.map(info => Ok(views.html.main(info.
attributes)))

        .recover {

        case t: Throwable =>

          Redirect(routes.Application.login())

      }

  }


  def login = Action.async {

    implicit request =>

      val openIdRequestURL: String = "https://me.yahoo.com"

      OpenID.redirectURL(

        openIdRequestURL,

        routes.Application.index.absoluteURL(),

        Seq("email" -> "http://schema.openid.net/contact/email",

          "name" -> "http://openid.net/schema/namePerson/first"))

        .map(url => Redirect(url))

        .recover { case t: Throwable => Ok(t.getMessage) }

    }

  }
```

In the preceding code snippet, the `login` method redirects the user to the Yahoo login page (refer to `https://me.yahoo.com`). Once the user logs in, he or she is asked if the user's profile can be shared by the application. If the user agrees, it redirects to `routes.Application.index.absoluteURL()`.

The `index` method expects data shared by the OpenID Provider (Yahoo, in our case) on a successful login. If it is not available, the user is redirected to the `login` method.

The third parameter for `OpenID.redirectURL` is a sequence of tuples which indicates the information required by the application (required attributes). The second element in each tuple label of the attribute property is requested using OpenID Attribute Exchange—it enables the transport of personal identity information. The first element in each tuple is the label with which the value for the attribute property should be mapped by the OpenID Provider in the callback request's `queryString`.

For example, the `http://openid.net/schema/namePerson/first` property represents the attribute property by its first name. On successful login, the value of this property and the label provided by the consumer are added to the `queryString` in the callback. So, `openid.ext1.value.name=firstName` is added to the login callback.

OAuth

According to `http://oauth.net/core/1.0/`, the definition of OAuth is as follows:

> *"OAuth authentication is the process in which Users grant access to their Protected Resources without sharing their credentials with the Consumer. OAuth uses Tokens generated by the Service Provider instead of the User's credentials in Protected Resources requests. The process uses two Token types:*
>
> *Request Token: Used by the Consumer to ask the User to authorize access to the Protected Resources. The User-authorized Request Token is exchanged for an Access Token, MUST only be used once, and MUST NOT be used for any other purpose. It is RECOMMENDED that Request Tokens have a limited lifetime.*
>
> *Access Token: Used by the Consumer to access the Protected Resources on behalf of the User. Access Tokens MAY limit access to certain Protected Resources, and MAY have a limited lifetime. Service Providers SHOULD allow Users to revoke Access Tokens. Only the Access Token SHALL be used to access the Protect Resources.*

> *OAuth Authentication is done in three steps:*
>
> *The Consumer obtains an unauthorized Request Token.*
>
> *The User authorizes the Request Token.*
>
> *The Consumer exchanges the Request Token for an Access Token."*

Exactly what and how much of it is accessible is decided solely by the service provider.

There are three versions of OAuth: 1.0, 1.0a, and 2.0. The first one (1.0) has some security issues and is not used anymore by service providers.

Play provides an API for using 1.0 and 1.0a and not for 2.0, since using this is a lot simpler. The API is documented at `https://www.playframework.com/documentation/2.3.x/api/scala/index.html#play.api.libs.oauth.package`.

Let's build an app to that utilizes a Twitter account to log in using Play's OAuth API.

Initially, we'll need to register the app at `https://apps.twitter.com/` using a Twitter account so that we have a valid consumer key and secret combination. After this, we can define the action as follows:

```
val KEY: ConsumerKey = ConsumerKey("myAppKey", "myAppSecret")
val TWITTER: OAuth = OAuth(ServiceInfo(
    "https://api.twitter.com/oauth/request_token",
    "https://api.twitter.com/oauth/access_token",
    "https://api.twitter.com/oauth/authorize", KEY),
    true)

def authenticate = Action { request =>
    TWITTER.retrieveRequestToken("http://localhost:9000/welcome")
match {
        case Right(t) => {
            Redirect(TWITTER.redirectUrl(t.token)).withSession("token" ->
t.token, "secret" -> t.secret)
        }
        case Left(e) => throw e
    }
}
```

OAuth is a Play helper class and has this signature:

```
OAuth(info: ServiceInfo, use10a: Boolean = true)
```

The parameter determines the version of OpenID. If it's set to `true`, it uses OpenID 1.0 or else, 1.0.

It provides these three methods:

- `redirectURL`: This fetches the URL string where a user should be redirected to authorize the application through the provider
- `retrieveRequestToken`: This fetches the request token from the provider
- `retrieveAccessToken`: This exchanges the request token for an access token

In the preceding action definition, we only use the provider to login; we cannot get any user details unless we do not exchange the authorized request token for an access token. To get the access token, we need the request token and `oauth_verifier`, which is provided by the service provider when granting the request token.

Using the Play OAuth API, redirecting after obtaining a request token adds `oauth_verifier` to the request query string. So, we should redirect to an action that attempts to obtain the access token and then store it, so that it is easily accessible for future requests. In this example, it's stored in the Session:

```
def authenticate = Action { request =>
    request.getQueryString("oauth_verifier").map { verifier =>
      val tokenPair = sessionTokenPair(request).get
      TWITTER.retrieveAccessToken(tokenPair, verifier) match {
        case Right(t) => {
          Redirect(routes.Application.welcome()).withSession("token"
            -> t.token, "secret" -> t.secret)
        }
        case Left(e) => throw e
      }
    }.getOrElse(
        TWITTER.retrieveRequestToken("http://localhost:9000/
          twitterLogin") match {
      case Right(rt) =>
        Redirect(TWITTER.redirectUrl(rt.token)).withSession("token"
          -> rt.token, "secret" -> rt.secret)
      case Left(e) => throw e
    })
  }

  private def sessionTokenPair(implicit request: RequestHeader):
Option[RequestToken] = {
    for {
      token <- request.session.get("token")
      secret <- request.session.get("secret")
    } yield {
      RequestToken(token, secret)
    }
```

```
    }

    def welcome = Action.async {
      implicit request =>
        sessionTokenPair match {
          case Some(credentials) => {
            WS.url("https://api.twitter.com/1.1/statuses/home_timeline.
              json")
              .sign(OAuthCalculator(KEY, credentials))
              .get()
              .map(result => Ok(result.json))
          }
          case _ => Future.successful(Redirect(routes.Application.
            authenticate()).withNewSession)
        }

    }
```

On successful login and authorization by the user, we fetch the status on a user's timeline and display it as JSON using the welcome action.

> There is no built-in support in Play for authentication using OAuth 2.0, CAS, SAML, or any other protocol. However, developers can choose to use a third-party plugin or library that suits their requirements. Some of them are Silhouette (http://silhouette.mohiva.com/v2.0), deadbolt-2 (https://github.com/schaloner/deadbolt-2), play-pac4j (https://github.com/pac4j/play-pac4j), and so on.

Summary

In this chapter, we learned about the WS (web service) plugin and the API exposed through it. We have also seen how to access a user's data from service providers using OpenID and OAuth 1.0a (since most service providers use either 1.0a or 2.0), with the help of the OpenID and OAuth APIs in Play.

In the next chapter, we will see how some of the modules provided by Play work and how we can build a custom module using them.

12
Play in Production

Application deployment, configurations, and so on are slightly different in a production environment since it is affected by various factors, such as security, load/traffic (which is expected to handle), network issues, and so on. In this chapter, we will see how to get our Play application up and running in production. This chapter covers the following topics:

- Deploying an application
- Configuring for production
- Enabling SSL
- Using a load balancer

Deploying a Play application

A Play Framework provides commands to package and deploy Play applications in production.

The `run` command, which we used earlier, starts the application in DEV mode and watches the code for changes. When there is a change in the code, the application is recompiled and reloaded. Being watchful is handy during development, but is an unnecessary overhead in production. Also, the default error pages shown in PROD mode are different from the ones shown in DEV mode, that is, they have less information about the errors that are occurring (for security reasons).

Let's look at the different ways in which we can deploy an application in production.

Using the start command

To start an application in PROD mode, we can use the start command:

```
[PlayScala] $ start
[info] Wrote /PlayScala/target/scala-2.10/playscala_2.10-1.0.pom


(Starting server. Type Ctrl+D to exit logs, the server will remain in
background)


Play server process ID is 24353
[info] play - Application started (Prod)
[info] play - Listening for HTTP on /0:0:0:0:0:0:0:0:9000
```

The process ID can be used later to stop the application. By pressing *Ctrl + D*, we do not lose the logs, since they are also captured in logs/application.log by default (that is, when there's been no change in the logger configuration).

The start command optionally accepts the port number at which the application should be deployed:

```
[PlayScala] $ start 9123
[info] Wrote /PlayScala/target/scala-2.10/playscala_2.10-1.0.pom


(Starting server. Type Ctrl+D to exit logs, the server will remain in
background)


Play server process ID is 12502
[info] play - Application started (Prod)
[info] play - Listening for HTTP on /0:0:0:0:0:0:0:0:9123
```

Using a distribution

Although the start command is good enough to deploy the application, in scenarios where a portable version of the application is required, it may not be sufficient. In this section, we will see how to build a standalone distribution of our application.

The Play Framework supports building a distribution of an application using the `sbt-native-packager` plugin (refer to `http://www.scala-sbt.org/sbt-native-packager/`). The plugin can be used to create the `.msi` (Windows), `.deb` (Debian), `.rpm` (Red Hat Package Manager), and `.zip` (universal) files, as well as the Docker images of our application. The plugin also supports defining settings for the package in the application's build file. Some of the settings are common while others are OS-specific. The common ones are shown in the following table:

Setting	Purpose	Default value
`packageName`	Name of the created output package without the extension	Project name transformed from mixed case and spaces to lowercase and dash-separated
`packageDescription`	The description of the package	Project name
`packageSummary`	Summary of the contents of a Linux package	Project name
`executableScriptName`	Name of the executing script	Project name transformed from mixed case and spaces to lowercase and dash-separated
`maintainer`	The name/e-mail address of a maintainer for the native package	

Now, let's see how we can build packages for different OSes and use them.

Universal distribution

A universal distribution is compatible with all/most operating systems. The generated packages are located at `projectHome/target/universal`. We can use any of the following commands to create a package as required:

- `universal:packageBin` – This command creates an `appname-appVersion.zip` file of the packaged application

- `universal:packageZipTarball` – This command creates an `appname-appVersion.tgz` file of the packaged application

- `universal:packageOsxDmg` – This command creates an `appname-appVersion.dmg` file of the packaged application (the command only works on OS X)

The `universal:packageZipTarball` command requires the `gzip`, `xz`, and `tar` command-line tools, while `universal:packageOsxDmg` requires OS X or systems installed with `hdiutil`.

To use the package built through these commands, extract the files and execute `bin/appname` for the Unix-based systems and `bin/appname.bat` for systems with Windows.

 In a Play application, we can use the `dist` command instead of `universal:packageBin`. The `dist` command deletes unnecessary intermediate files created while packaging the application using the `universal:packageBin` command.

Debian distribution

We can create a distribution that can be installed on Debian-based systems using the `debian:packageBin` command. The `.deb` file is located at `projectHome/target`.

 To build the Debian package, the value for `packageDescription` in the Debian setting should be set in the `build` file. Other Debian package settings can also be set in the `build` file.

After packaging, we can install the application using `dpkg-deb`:

```
projectHome$ sudo dpkg -i target/appname-appVersion.deb
```

Once it's installed, we can start the application by executing this:

```
$ sudo appname
```

The rpm distribution

An `rpm` package of the application can be created using the `rpm:packageBin` command. Some of the settings available for the `rpm` package are shown in the following table:

Setting	Purpose
rpmVendor	Name of the vendor for this `rpm` package
rpmLicense	License of the code within the `rpm` package
rpmUrl	URL to include in the `rpm` package

Setting	Purpose
rpmDescription	Description of this rpm package
rpmRelease	Special release number for this rpm package

 The values for rpmVendor in rpm, packageSummary in rpm, and packageDescription in rpm must be set in the build file to successfully create an rpm package of the application where rpm is the scope, for example the name in rpm:= "SampleProject".

Once the rpm package is generated, we can install it using yum or an equivalent tool:

```
projectHome$ sudo yum install target/appname-appVersion.rpm
```

After the installation is completed, we can start the application by executing this:

```
$ sudo appname
```

Windows distribution

A Windows installer of the application, appname-appVersion.msi, can be created using the windows:packageBin command. The file is located at projectHome/target.

Configuring for production

The Play Framework understands that applications may require changes in configuration prior to deployment in production. To simplify deploying, the command to deploy the application also accepts application-level configurations as arguments:

```
[PlayScala] $ start -Dapplication.secret=S3CR3T
[info] Wrote /PlayScala/target/scala-2.10/playscala_2.10-1.0.pom


(Starting server. Type Ctrl+D to exit logs, the server will remain in
background)


Play server process ID is 14904
```

Let's change the application's HTTP port as follows:

```
#setting http port to 1234
[PlayScala] $ start -Dhttp.port=1234
```

In some projects, the production and development configuration are maintained in two separate files. We could either pass one or more configurations or a different file altogether. There are three ways of specifying a configuration file explicitly. It can be achieved by using one of the following options:

- `config.resource`: This option is used when the file is within the class path (a file in `application/conf`)
- `config.file`: This option is used when the file is available on the local filesystem but not bundled with the application's resources
- `config.url`: This option is used when the file is to be loaded from a URL

Suppose our application uses `conf/application-prod.conf` in production, we can specify the file as follows:

```
[PlayScala] $ start -Dconfig.resource=application-prod.conf
```

Similarly, we can also modify the logger configuration by replacing the `config` key with `logger`:

```
[PlayScala] $ start -Dlogger.resource=logger-prod.xml
```

We can also configure the underlying Netty server by passing the settings as arguments and this not possible through `application.conf`. The following table lists some of the settings related to the server that can be configured in one or more ways.

The properties related to the address and port are as follows:

Property	Purpose	Default value
http.address	The address at which the application will be deployed	0.0.0.0
http.port	The port at which the application will be available	9000
https.port	The `sslPort` port at which the application will be available	

The properties related to the HTTP requests (`HttpRequestDecoder`) are as follows:

Property	Purpose	Default value
http.netty. maxInitialLineLength	The maximum length of the initial line (for example, GET / HTTP/1.0)	4096
http.netty. maxHeaderSize	The maximum length of all the headers combined together	8192

Property	Purpose	Default value
`http.netty.` `maxChunkSize`	The maximum length of the body or each chunk of it. If the length of the body exceeds this value, the content will be split into chunks of this size or less (in case of the last one). If the request sends the chunked data and the length of a chunk exceeds this value, it will be split into smaller chunks.	8192

The properties related to the TCP socket options are shown in the following table:

Property	Purpose	Default
`http.netty.option.` `backlog`	The maximum size for queued incoming connections	
`http.netty.option.` `reuseAddress`	Reuse address	
`http.netty.option.` `receiveBufferSize`	The size of the socket that receives a buffer	
`http.netty.option.` `sendBufferSize`	The size of the socket that sends a buffer	
`http.netty.option.` `child.keepAlive`	Keeps connections alive	`False`
`http.netty.option.` `child.soLinger`	Lingers on closing if the data is present	Negative integer (disabled)
`http.netty.option.` `tcpNoDelay`	Disables Nagle's algorithm. TCP/IP uses an algorithm known as Nagle's algorithm to coalesce short segments and improve network efficiency.	`False`
`http.netty.option.` `trafficClass`	The **Type of Service** (**ToS**) octet in the **Internet Protocol** (IP) header.	0

Enabling SSL

There are two ways of enabling SSL for our application. We can either serve an HTTPS application by the providing the required configuration for it on start, or by proxying the requests through an SSL-enabled web server. In this section, we will see how the first option can be used and the latter will be covered in the next section.

We can choose to run both the HTTP and HTTPS versions or just opt for one of them using the `http.port` and `https.port` settings. By default, HTTPS is disabled and we can enable it by specifying `https.port` as follows:

```
#setting https port to 1234
[PlayScala] $ start -Dhttps.port=1234
```

```
#disabling http port and setting https port to 1234
[PlayScala] $ start -Dhttp.port=disabled -Dhttps.port=1234
```

Play generates self-signed certificates if we do not provide them, and starts the application with SSL enabled in it. However, these certificates are unsuitable for an actual application and we need to specify the details of the key store using the following settings:

Property	Purpose	Default value
`https.keyStore`	The path to the key store containing a private key and certificate	This value is dynamically generated
`https.keyStoreType`	The key store type	**JavaKeyStore (JKS)**
`https.keyStorePassword`	The password	Blank password
`https.keyStoreAlgorithm`	The key store algorithm	The platform's default algorithm

In addition to this, we can also specify `SSLEngine` through the `play.http.sslengineprovider` setting. The prerequisite for this is that the custom `SSLEngine` should implement the `play.server.api.SSLEngineProvider` trait.

> It is recommended to use JDK 1.8 when a Play application with SSL enabled is running in production, since Play uses some of the features of JDK 1.8 to facilitate it. If using JDK 1.8 is not feasible, a reverse proxy with SSL enabled should be used instead. Refer to `https://www.playframework.com/documentation/2.3.x/ConfiguringHttps` for more details.

Using a load balancer

Websites that deal with huge traffic generally use a technique called load balancing to improve the availability and responsiveness of applications. A load balancer distributes incoming traffic among multiple servers hosting same content. The distribution of load is determined by various scheduler algorithms.

In this section, we will see how to add a load balancer in front of our application servers (assuming that they are running on the IPs `127.0.0.1`, `127.0.0.2`, and `127.0.0.3` on the port `9000`) using different HTTP web servers.

Apache HTTP

The Apache HTTP server provides a secure, efficient, and extensible server that supports HTTP services. The Apache HTTP server can be used as a load balancer through its `mod_proxy` and `mod_proxy_balance` modules.

To use Apache HTTP as a load balancer, `mod_proxy` and `mod_proxy_balancer` have to be present in the server. To set up the load balancer, all we need to do is update `/etc/httpd/conf/httpd.conf`.

Let's update the configuration step by step:

1. Declare `VirtualHost`:

   ```
   <VirtualHost *:80>
   </VirtualHost>
   ```

2. Disable the forward proxy for `VirtualHost` so that our server cannot be used for masking the identities of clients from the source servers:

   ```
   ProxyRequests off
   ```

3. Instead of a document root, we should add a proxy with balancer identifier and `BalanceMembers`. Also, if we want to use the **round-robin** strategy, we also need to set it as `lbmethod` (**load balancing method**):

   ```
   <Proxy balancer://app>
       BalancerMember http://127.0.0.1:9000
           BalancerMember http://127.0.0.2:9000
           BalancerMember http://127.0.0.3:9000
       ProxySet lbmethod=byrequests
   </Proxy>
   ```

4. Now, we need to add the access permissions for the proxy, which should be accessible to everyone:

```
Order Deny,Allow
Deny from none
Allow from all
```

5. Finally, we need to map the proxy to the path that we want to load the application on the server to. This can be done with a single line:

```
ProxyPass / balancer://app/
```

The configuration that needs to be added to the Apache HTTP configuration file is as follows:

```
<VirtualHost *:80>
        ProxyPreserveHost On
        ProxyRequests off
        <Proxy balancer://app>

                BalancerMember http://127.0.0.1:9000
                BalancerMember http://127.0.0.2:9000
                BalancerMember http://127.0.0.3:9000
                Order Deny,Allow
                Deny from none
                Allow from all

                ProxySet lbmethod=byrequests
        </Proxy>
        ProxyPass / balancer://app/
</VirtualHost>
```

To enable SSL, we will need to add the following code to the `VirtualHost` definition:

```
SSLEngine on
SSLCertificateFile /path/to/domain.com.crt
SSLCertificateKeyFile /path/to/domain.com.key
```

 This configuration has been tried on Apache/2.4.10 on July 31, 2014.

For more information on Apache HTTP's `mod_proxy` module, refer to
http://httpd.apache.org/docs/2.2/mod/mod_proxy.html.

The nginx server

The **nginx** server is a high performance HTTP server and a reverse proxy as well. It is also an IMAP/POP3 proxy server. We can configure nginx to act as a load balancer using two modules—proxy and upstream. These two modules are part of the nginx core and are available by default.

The nginx configuration file, nginx.conf, is generally located at /etc/nginx. Let's update it to use nginx as a load balancer for our application step by step:

1. First, we need to define an upstream module for our cluster of application servers. The syntax is as follows:

```
upstream <group> {
<loadBalancingMethod>;
server <server1>;
server <server2>;
}
```

The default load balancing method is round-robin. So, we need not specify it explicitly when we wish to use it. Now, for our application, the upstream module will be as follows:

```
upstream app {
    server 127.0.0.1:9000;
    server 127.0.0.2:9000;
    server 127.0.0.3:9000;
}
```

2. Now, all that we need to do is proxy all the requests. To do this, we must update the server module's location module:

```
server {
    listen       80 default_server;
    server_name  localhost;
    ...
    location / {
        proxy_pass http://app;
        proxy_set_header Host $host;
    }
}
```

The nginx server also supports proxying **WebSocket**. To enable WebSocket connections, we need to add two headers to the `location` module. So, if our Play application uses WebSocket, we can define the `location` module as follows:

```
location / {
    proxy_pass http://app;
    proxy_set_header Host $host;
    proxy_http_version 1.1;
    proxy_set_header Upgrade $http_upgrade;
    proxy_set_header Connection "upgrade";
}
```

To enable SSL, we need to add the following settings to the server definition:

```
ssl_certificate        /path/to/domain.com.crt;
ssl_certificate_key path/to/domain.com.key;
```

> This configuration has been tested on nginx/1.4.7.
>
> Refer to the nginx documentation at `http://nginx.org/en/ docs/http/load_balancing.html#nginx_load_balancing_ configuration` for more details.

lighttpd

The `lighttpd` server is a lightweight web server designed and optimized for high performance environments. All the utilities that may be required are available as modules and can be included as per our requirements. We can set `lighttpd` as a frontend server for our Play application using the `mod_proxy` module. We need to make a few configuration changes to achieve this. They are as follows:

1. Update the `lighttpd.conf` file (generally located at `/etc/lighttpd/`) to load additional modules.

2. By default, loading modules is disabled. This can be enabled by uncommenting this line:

   ```
   include "modules.conf"
   ```

3. Update `modules.conf` (located in the same directory as `lighttpd.conf`) to load the `mod_proxy` module.

4. By default, only `mod_access` is enabled. Update `server.modules` to the following code:

```
server.modules = (
    "mod_access",
    "mod_proxy"
)
```

5. Now, enable loading the settings for `mod_proxy` by uncommenting this line:

```
include "conf.d/proxy.conf"
```

6. Update the `proxy.conf` file (generally located at `/etc/lighttpd/conf.d/`) with the server proxy configuration. The q module has only three settings:

    ○   `proxy.debug`: This setting enables/disables the log level

    ○   `proxy.balance`: This setting is a load balancing algorithm (round-robin, hash, and fair)

    ○   `proxy.server`: This setting is where requests are sent

    The expected format of defining a `proxy.server` setting is as follows:

```
( <extension> =>
    ( [ <name> => ]
    ( "host" => <string> ,
        "port" => <integer> ),
    ( "host" => <string> ,
        "port" => <integer> )
    ),
    <extension> => ...
)
```

    The terms in this code are explained as follows:

    ○   `<extension>`: This term is the file extension or prefix (if started with `"/"`); empty quotes, `""`, match all the requests

    ○   `<name>`:This term is the optional name that shows up in the generated statistics of `mod_status`

    ○   `host`: This term is used to specify the IP address of the proxy server

    ○   `port`: This term is used to set the TCP port on its corresponding host (the default value is `80`)

7. Update the proxy settings as required:

```
server.modules += ( "mod_proxy" )
proxy.balance = "round-robin"
proxy.server = ( "" =>
    ( "app" =>
        (
            "host" => "127.0.0.1",
            "port" => 9000
        ),
        (
            "host" => "127.0.0.2",
            "port" => 9000
        ),
        (
            "host" => "127.0.0.3",
            "port" => 9000
        )
    )
)
```

This configuration has been tried on lighttpd/1.4.35 on March 12, 2014.

For more information on the configuration settings of mod_proxy, refer to http://redmine.lighttpd.net/projects/lighttpd/wiki/Docs_ModProxy.

High Availability Proxy

High Availability Proxy (HAProxy) offers high availability, load balancing, and proxying for TCP and HTTP-based applications. We can set HAProxy as a load balancer by updating the haproxy.cfg configuration file (it is generally located at /etc/haproxy/).

Let's make the required configuration changes step by step:

1. First, we need to define the backend cluster. The syntax for defining a backend is as follows:

```
backend <name>
balance    <load balance method>
server <sname> <ip>:<port>
server     <sname> <ip>:<port>
```

2. So, the backend for our application will be as follows:

```
backend app
    balance      roundrobin
    server   app1 127.0.0.1:9000
    server   app1 127.0.0.2:9000
    server   app1 127.0.0.3:9000
```

3. Now, we just need to point requests to the backend cluster. We can do this by updating the frontend section:

```
frontend  main *:80
default_backend              app
```

No additional configuration is required for an application using WebSockets.

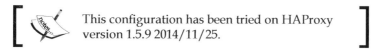

This configuration has been tried on HAProxy version 1.5.9 2014/11/25.

Troubleshooting

These are some corner cases you might encounter:

- We need to deploy our application on Tomcat. How can we package the application as WAR?

  Although this is not supported by default in Play, we can use the `play2-war-plugin` module (refer to `https://github.com/play2war/play2-war-plugin/`) to achieve this.

- Is there a simpler way to deploy the application on PaaS?

  Deploying Play applications on Heroku, Clever Cloud, Cloud Foundry and/or AppFog are documented at `https://www.playframework.com/documentation/2.3.x/DeployingCloud`.

Summary

In this chapter, we saw how to deploy a Play application in production. While deploying it, we saw the different packaging options (such as `rpm`, `deb`, `zip`, `windows`, and so on) available by default. We also saw different configuration settings, such as the HTTP port, maximum size of the request header, and so on, which we can specify when starting the application in production. We also discussed how to send requests to the application using a reverse proxy.

In the next chapter, we will discuss how the Play plugins work, and how we can build custom Play plugins to meet different requirements.

13
Writing Play Plugins

In order to make our applications manageable, we break them down into independent modules. These modules can also be extracted into individual projects/libraries.

A Play plugin is nothing but another module with an additional ability — of binding tasks before starting, on starting and/or stopping a Play application. In this chapter, we will see how to write custom plugins.

In this chapter, we will cover the following topics:

- Plugin definition
- Plugin declaration
- Exposing services through plugins
- Tips for writing a plugin

Plugin definition

A Play plugin can be defined by extending `play.api.plugin`, which is defined as follows:

```
trait Plugin {

  //Called when the application starts.
  def onStart() {}

  // Called when the application stops.
  def onStop() {}

  // Is the plugin enabled?
  def enabled: Boolean = true
}
```

Now, we might be in a situation where we need to send an e-mail when an application is started or stopped so that the administrator can later use this time interval to monitor the application's performance and check why it stopped. We could define a plugin to do this for us:

```scala
class NotifierPlugin(app:Application) extends Plugin{

  private def notify(adminId:String,status:String):Unit = {

    val time = new Date()

    val msg = s"The app has been $status at $time"

    //send email to admin with the msg

    log.info(msg)

  }



  override def onStart() {

    val emailId =
      app.configuration.getString("notify.admin.id").get

    notify(emailId,"started")

  }



  override def onStop() {

    val emailId =
      app.configuration.getString("notify.admin.id").get

    notify(emailId,"stopped")

  }



  override def enabled: Boolean = true

}
```

We can also define plugins that make use of other libraries. We might need to build a plugin that builds a connection pool to `Cassandra` (a NoSQL database) on startup and allows users to use this pool later on. To build this plugin, we will use the `cassandra-driver` for Java. Our plugin will then be as follows:

```scala
class CassandraPlugin(app: Application) extends Plugin {

  private var _helper: Option[CassandraConnection] = None

  def helper = _helper.getOrElse(throw new
    RuntimeException("CassandraPlugin error: CassandraHelper
      initialization failed"))

  override def onStart() = {

    val appConfig =
      app.configuration.getConfig("cassandraPlugin").get
    val appName: String =
      appConfig.getString("appName").getOrElse
        ("appWithCassandraPlugin")

    val hosts: Array[java.lang.String] =
      appConfig.getString("host").getOrElse("localhost").split
        (",").map(_.trim)
    val port: Int = appConfig.getInt("port").getOrElse(9042)

    val cluster = Cluster.builder()
      .addContactPoints(hosts: _*)
      .withPort(port).build()

    _helper = try {
      val session = cluster.connect()
      Some(CassandraConnection(hosts, port, cluster, session))
    } catch {
      case e: NoHostAvailableException =>
        val msg =
          s"""Failed to initialize CassandraPlugin.
             |Please check if Cassandra is accessible at
             | ${hosts.head}:$port or update
               configuration""".stripMargin
        throw app.configuration.globalError(msg)
    }
  }

  override def onStop() = {
```

```
        helper.session.close()
        helper.cluster.close()
    }

    override def enabled = true
}
```

Here, `CassandraConnection` is defined as follows:

```
private[plugin] case class CassandraConnection(hosts:
    Array[java.lang.String],
    port: Int,
    cluster: Cluster,
session: Session)
```

The `cassandra-driver` node is declared as a library dependency and its classes are imported where they're required.

 The dependency on Play in the `build` definition of the plugin should be marked as provided, since the application using the plugin will already have a dependency on Play, as shown here:

```
libraryDependencies ++= Seq(
    "com.datastax.cassandra" % "cassandra-driver-core" %
        "2.0.4",
    "com.typesafe.play" %% "play" % "2.3.0" % "provided" )
```

Plugin declaration

Now that we have defined a plugin, let's see how the Play Framework identifies and enables it for the application. `ApplicationProvider` for the production and development mode (static and reloadable applications, respectively) both rely on `DefaultApplication`, which is defined as follows:

```
class DefaultApplication(
    override val path: File,
    override val classloader: ClassLoader,
    override val sources: Option[SourceMapper],
    override val mode: Mode.Mode) extends Application with
        WithDefaultConfiguration with WithDefaultGlobal with
            WithDefaultPlugins
```

The `trait WithDefaultPlugins` line is responsible for binding the plugins to application's life cycle. It is defined as follows:

```
trait WithDefaultPlugins {
  self: Application =>
  private[api] def pluginClasses: Seq[String] = {
    import scala.collection.JavaConverters._
    val PluginDeclaration = """([0-9_]+):(.*)""".r
    val pluginFiles =
      self.classloader.getResources("play.plugins").asScala.toList
        ++
          self.classloader.getResources("conf/play.plugins").
            asScala.toList

    pluginFiles.distinct.map { plugins =>
      PlayIO.readUrlAsString(plugins).split("\n").map(_.replaceAll
        ("#.*$", "").trim).filterNot(_.isEmpty).map {
        case PluginDeclaration(priority, className) =>
          (priority.toInt, className)
      }
    }.flatten.sortBy(_._1).map(_._2)

  }
  ...
}
```

So, we should declare our plugin class in a file with the `play.plugins` name. All the plugin declarations obtained from one or more `play.plugins` files are combined and sorted. Each declared plugin has a priority assigned to it, which is used for sorting. Once sorted, the plugins are loaded in order prior to the application's startup.

The priorities should be set based on the dependencies of a plugin. The suggested priorities are as follows:

- `100`: This priority is set when a plugin has no dependencies, such as the messages plugin (used for `i18n`)

- `200`: This priority is set for the plugins that create and manage the DB connection pools

- `300-500`: This priority is set for the plugins that depend on a database, such as JPA, Ebean, and evolutions

 `10000` is reserved for a global plugin intentionally so that it loads after all the other plugins have been loaded. This allows developers to use other plugins in the global object without additional configuration.

The default `play.plugins` file just has a basic plugin declaration:

```
1:play.core.system.MigrationHelper
100:play.api.i18n.DefaultMessagesPlugin
1000:play.api.libs.concurrent.AkkaPlugin
10000:play.api.GlobalPlugin
```

A few more plugin declarations from the Play modules are as follows:

```
200:play.api.db.BoneCPPlugin
500:play.api.db.evolutions.EvolutionsPlugin
600:play.api.cache.EhCachePlugin
700:play.api.libs.ws.ning.NingWSPlugin
```

 Generally, Play plugins need to be specified as library dependencies in the application's `build` definition. Some plugins are bundled with a `play.plugins` file. However, for those without it, we will need to set the priority in our application's `conf/play.plugins` file.

Exposing services through plugins

Some plugins need to provide users with helper methods to simplify transactions, whereas others need not do anything besides some tasks to be added in the application's life cycle. For example, our `NotifierPlugin` just sends e-mails on start and stop. Then, the methods of our `CassandraPlugin` can be accessed using the `plugin` method of `play.api.Application`:

```
object CassandraHelper {
  private val casPlugin =
    Play.application.plugin[CassandraPlugin].get

  //complete DB transactions with the connection pool started
    through the plugin
  def executeStmt(stmt:String) = {
    casPlugin.session.execute(stmt)
  }

}
```

Alternatively, the plugin can also provide a helper object:

```
object Cassandra {
  private val casPlugin =
    Play.application.plugin[CassandraPlugin].get

  private val cassandraHelper = casPlugin.helper

  /**
   * gets the Cassandra hosts provided in the configuration
   */
  def hosts: Array[java.lang.String] = cassandraHelper.hosts

  /**
   * gets the port number on which Cassandra is running from the
     configuration
   */
  def port: Int = cassandraHelper.port

  /**
   * gets a reference of the started Cassandra cluster
   * The cluster is built with the configured set of initial
     contact points
   * and policies at startup
   */
  def cluster: Cluster = cassandraHelper.cluster

  /**
   * gets a reference of the started Cassandra session
   * A new session is created on the cluster at startup
   */
  def session: Session = cassandraHelper.session

  /**
   * executes CQL statements available in given file.
   * Empty lines or lines starting with `#` are ignored.
   * Each statement can extend over multiple lines and must end
     with a semi-colon.
   * @param fileName - name of the file
   */
  def loadCQLFile(fileName: String): Unit = {
    Util.loadScript(fileName, cassandraHelper.session)
  }

}
```

A list of available modules is maintained at `https://www.playframework.com/documentation/2.3.x/Modules`.

Tips for writing a plugin

Here are some tips for writing a plugin:

- Before you start writing a plugin, check if you really need one to solve your problem. If your problem does not require meddling with the application's life cycle, it's better to write a library.

- While writing/updating a plugin, simultaneously build an example Play application that uses the plugin. This will allow you to check the functionality of it thoroughly with only the additional overheads of publishing the plugin locally for every change made.

- If the plugin exposes some services, try to provide a helper object. This makes it easier to maintain the API's consistency and also simplifies the developer experience.

  For example, most of the plugins provided by Play (such as `akka`, `jdbc`, `ws`, and so on) provide helper objects through which the API is available. Internal changes to the plugin do not affect the public API exposed through these objects.

- If and where possible, try and back up the plugin with sufficient tests.

- Document the API and/or special cases. This might come in handy in future for everyone who uses the plugin.

Summary

The Play plugins provide us with the flexibility to perform specific tasks at a desired stage in the application's life cycle. Play has some plugins that are commonly required by most applications, such as web services, authentication, and so on. We discussed how the Play plugins work and how we can build custom plugins to meet different requirements.

Index

A

Action
  Asynchronous Actions 33-36
  composition 42
  defining 19, 20
  troubleshooting 48, 49
  with parameters 20-22
Action composition
  about 42
  and filters, differentiating 45
  customized requests 45-47
  need for 43, 44
  user object, need for 47
Actor Model 161
Actors
  using without Iteratees, for
      WebSocket 168, 169
Akka Actors
  about 162, 164
  URL 164
Anorm
  about 108-111
  URL 108
Apache HTTP 231, 232
AppFog
  URL 237
application life cycle
  about 144
  ApplicationProvider,
      implementing 145, 146
  running state 144, 145
  specifications 146-150
  stopped state 144, 145
ApplicationProvider, implementations
  ReloadableApplication 145

  StaticApplication 145
  TestApplication 145
Artist model 17-19
assets 59-62
Asynchronous Actions 33-36

B

Basic authentication
  URL 216
BoneCP
  URL 106

C

Cache API 119-123
client-side libraries 62
Concurrent object
  about 135
  broadcast 136
  unicast 135
content negotiation 36-39
controller, unit testing
  about 179, 180
  dependency injection used 182-185
  traits used 180, 181

D

Data Definition Language (DDL) 112
Data Manipulation Language (DML) 112
data streams
  handling 127-129
Debian distribution 226
debugging
  about 197
  Play application 197

Thank you for buying
Mastering Play Framework for Scala

About Packt Publishing

Packt, pronounced 'packed', published its first book, *Mastering phpMyAdmin for Effective MySQL Management*, in April 2004, and subsequently continued to specialize in publishing highly focused books on specific technologies and solutions.

Our books and publications share the experiences of your fellow IT professionals in adapting and customizing today's systems, applications, and frameworks. Our solution-based books give you the knowledge and power to customize the software and technologies you're using to get the job done. Packt books are more specific and less general than the IT books you have seen in the past. Our unique business model allows us to bring you more focused information, giving you more of what you need to know, and less of what you don't.

Packt is a modern yet unique publishing company that focuses on producing quality, cutting-edge books for communities of developers, administrators, and newbies alike. For more information, please visit our website at www.packtpub.com.

About Packt Open Source

In 2010, Packt launched two new brands, Packt Open Source and Packt Enterprise, in order to continue its focus on specialization. This book is part of the Packt Open Source brand, home to books published on software built around open source licenses, and offering information to anybody from advanced developers to budding web designers. The Open Source brand also runs Packt's Open Source Royalty Scheme, by which Packt gives a royalty to each open source project about whose software a book is sold.

Writing for Packt

We welcome all inquiries from people who are interested in authoring. Book proposals should be sent to author@packtpub.com. If your book idea is still at an early stage and you would like to discuss it first before writing a formal book proposal, then please contact us; one of our commissioning editors will get in touch with you.

We're not just looking for published authors; if you have strong technical skills but no writing experience, our experienced editors can help you develop a writing career, or simply get some additional reward for your expertise.

Learning Play! Framework 2

ISBN: 978-1-78216-012-0   Paperback: 290 pages

Start developing awesome web applications with this friendly, practical guide to the Play! Framework

1. While driving in Java, tasks are also presented in Scala – a great way to be introduced to this amazing language.

2. Create a fully-fledged, collaborative web application – starting from ground zero; all layers are presented in a pragmatic way.

3. Gain the advantages associated with developing a fully integrated web framework.

Play Framework Cookbook

ISBN: 978-1-84951-552-8   Paperback: 292 pages

Over 60 incredibly effective recipes to take you under the hood and leverage advanced concepts of the Play framework

1. Make your application more modular, by introducing you to the world of modules.

2. Keep your application up and running in production mode, from setup to monitoring it appropriately.

3. Integrate play applications into your CI environment.

4. Keep performance high by using caching.

Please check **www.PacktPub.com** for information on our titles

Play Framework Essentials

ISBN: 978-1-78398-240-0   Paperback: 200 pages

An intuitive guide to creating easy-to-build scalable web applications using the Play framework

1. Master the complexity of designing a modern and scalable Web application by leveraging the Play Framework stack.

2. The key concepts of the framework are illustrated with both Scala and Java code examples.

3. A step-by-step guide with code examples based on a sample application built from the ground up, providing the practical skills required to develop Scala- or Java-based applications.

Play! Framework for Web Application Development [Video]

ISBN: 978-1-78216-548-4   Duration: 02:07 hours

Leverage the awesome Play! Framework to develop Java web applications

1. Learn by example how to create a WebApp and re-utilize code with Play! 2.

2. Discover quick and productive ways to implement your ideas.

3. Create your own APIs and make your site beautiful with Bootstrap.

Please check **www.PacktPub.com** for information on our titles

Made in the USA
San Bernardino, CA
20 April 2016